FOR EVERY SEASON

there is an hors d'oeuvre

Brio Press
12 South Sixth Street #1250
Minneapolis, Minnesota 55402
www.briobooks.com

Manufactured in the United States of America

10 9 8 7 6 5 4 3 2 1

Edited by Cindy Choate
Book Design by Brio | Anthony Sclavi Minneapolis, MN
Photography by Mark Choate

ISBN 13: 978-1-937061-96-8
Library of Congress Control Number: 2011940306

FOR EVERY SEASON

there is an hors d'oeuvre

LINDA STEIDEL

Photography by Mark Choate

SUMMER

AUTUMN

WINTER

SPRING

acknowledgements

Writing a good cookbook is a team sport. That's one thing I've learned. The book you are holding reflects the hard work of some very talented people. I'm just the lucky one who gets to put her name on the cover.

Will Reynolds, my publisher, is a valuable guide through the literary maze. Everyone at Brio Books has consistently been there for us. To my friends at Williams-Sonoma, thank you for your caring support. Our designer, Anthony Sclavi, keeps setting the bar higher with each book. Anthony, I don't know how you do that, but please, don't stop! I'm very blessed to have Linda Fasoli as our business manager. Linda is the protector of our little enterprise. She "has my back". As editor, Cindy, the last person to release the book to the printer, is invaluable. She also acts as stand in for the reader, questioning just about everything. Then, there is Mark. Again you have accompanied each recipe with an image you can almost taste. I say almost, so, Mark, keep trying.

Finally, I want to say thank you to my trusted corps of loyal, supporting, loving students. Your belief in me got me started, and keeps me going. For each of you, I will be eternally grateful.

Love,
Linda

Hors d'oeuvre & Canapés by James Beard

This is a quote from the first book written by James Beard in 1940. He was in the early years of his long, celebrated career. This landmark book remains a surprisingly rich resource for any party host.

James Beard knew that the hors d'oeuvre was what comes before the meal. It is intended to excite the mind and tease the appetite without dulling the desire for the food that is still to come. In 1962 he set out to re-edit the 1940 edition and realized just how timeless it was. When Beard talked food, he talked in timeless truths.

Mr. Beard had a few simple rules for the perfect cocktail party.

1. Don't invite more people than your living room will hold, and don't keep adding to the list.
2. Don't make your friends guinea pigs. The time to try out a new drink or hors d'oeuvre is with some kind and understanding friend.
3. Don't forget how important the food is. No matter how simple it should show some degree of imagination.
4. Don't forget it is a festive event; make your house show it.
5. Do remember to see that the guests are well cared for.

These were a great guide for entertaining in 1940 and still are perfect for 2011, seventy-one years later. How lucky we are to learn from the pioneers who paved the way for all of us.

Thank you, Mr. Beard!
Linda

> **"Each morsel is delicious and stimulating to the appetite, for it is flavored with goodwill and love and understanding."**

the lowly hors d'oeuvre

When you think about it, you have to feel sorry for the poor little hors d'oeuvre. Look at these walking orders!

- As the opening act, set the bar high, raise expectations, but don't dare outshine the main course or dessert finale. Be stunning, but not memorable!
- Be extremely satisfying. Be amazing. Be a delight that the guests can't get enough of. Yet, under no circumstances be filling, even if the guests take numerous servings.
- Be neat enough to be eaten with one hand, while the guest holds a drink in the other.
- Drip, ooze with flavor, but do not stain my expensive carpet!!
- Don't even think about joining all of the other wonderful dishes at the dining table.
- While you must be a star, you are still banished from the main tent.

Gosh, if I were an hors d'oeuvre I would freeze in sheer panic. The hors d'oeuvre's is a tough act. No other dish has such contradicting stipulations as does our opening act. So, this one deserves special attention. With that in mind, I think you'll find this book of hors d'oeuvres a worthy companion in planning and creating a dining experience that will be long remembered (well . . . maybe not the hors d'oeuvres).

The Party Perfect

This challenge is presented to me every holiday season. More and more of us want to be able to accommodate more guests, but do not have the room, dishes, glasses, or linens to do it. I think I have the solution. Let's start at the beginning.

We need small, savory and in most cases, one or two bite hors d'oeuvres. It is critical that they taste as good as they look. When planning what to have, think in terms of a complete menu. Include a variety of choices. Chicken, seafood, meat, vegetarian, cheese and a sweet. Keep it simple. Think about dishes that you love and condense them into hors d'oeuvre sizes. For example, small pots of mac & cheese or your favorite meatloaf made in a mini-muffin tin. You'll find lots of good ideas in this book.

There are a few guide lines to follow that might help. These are general rules, but will help you when planning your party.

1. 5 to 6 different hors d'oeuvres with a variety of meats, vegetables and cheeses.
2. 3 of each hors d'oeuvre per person. I know, not every person will eat 3 of each but, someone will take 7 of one. Best to be prepared.
3. Make sure people know what is in the hors d'oeuvre. Need to avoid allergy attacks.
4. Better to have more than you need, running out of the most popular one—not good.
5. If you are stressed, everyone at the party will know. Make as much ahead of time as you possibly can and have a glass of wine before your guests arrive.
6. Finish with a sweet. Mini cupcakes or cookies work well.
7. Set the mood. Lots of candles, flowers and great music.

This book is meant to be a handbook that will guide, instruct and inspire you with recipes and ideas for presentation and serving. I wanted to combine international flavors and inspirations from my trips with American favorites to create a range of reliable and simple recipes. Finally, just remember . . . if you are having fun, your guests will have fun.

Relax and enjoy the party!

SUMMER

Asparagus and Prosciutto Bundles

24 thin asparagus spears
2 ½ ounces soft fresh goat cheese, at room temperature
2 tablespoons chopped fresh basil
1 tablespoon toasted pine nuts, chopped
1 tablespoon water
1 teaspoon grated orange peel
2 ounces thinly sliced prosciutto, cut into 24 4x1-inch strips

Makes 24

1. Cut bottom 2 inches from asparagus. Peel stalks another two inches from tips.
2. Cook asparagus in large pan of boiling water until crisp tender. Drain. Transfer asparagus to paper towels and drain well. Mix goat cheese, basil, pine nuts, water and orange peel in small bowl to blend. Season with salt and pepper.
3. Spread scant 1 teaspoon filling over each prosciutto strip. Arrange 1 asparagus spear on top of filling at the short end of the piece of prosciutto. Roll up prosciutto, enclosing asparagus. Press to seal.
4. Place on platter and garnish with fresh basil leaves. (Can be made 1 day ahead; Cover, chill.)

Gazpacho Gelées with Avocado Cream

1 cup drained canned tomatoes, chopped
1 cup peeled, seeded and chopped cucumber
1 cup peeled and chopped red pepper
2 tablespoons red wine vinegar
½ teaspoon garlic, grated
Dash of hot sauce
Pinch of ground cumin
Salt
1 ½ teaspoons powdered unflavored gelatin
2 avocados, seeded, peeled and chopped
½ cup water
2 tablespoons fresh lime juice
4 teaspoons olive oil

Serves 8

I serve this two ways. It is great as an hors d'oeuvre in mini parfait glasses or shot glasses, or on top of butter lettuce as part of a summer salad.

1. In a blender, purée the tomatoes with the cucumber, red pepper, vinegar, garlic, hot sauce and cumin. Pass through a fine strainer into a glass measuring cup. Season with salt.
2. Transfer half of the mixture to a small saucepan. Sprinkle the gelatin evenly over the mixture and let stand for 5 minutes. Cook the mixture over moderate heat until the gelatin is melted, about 1 minute.
3. Stir in the remaining tomato mixture. Pour into 8 small glass bowls or ramekins and refrigerate until firm, about 1 hour.
4. Meanwhile, clean out the blender, then purée the chopped avocado with the water, lime juice and olive oil. Season with salt. Spoon the avocado cream over each gelée and serve.

Grilled Tuscan Bread with Tomato, Feta & Pesto

1 loaf Tuscan ciabatta or flat bread, cut into thin slices and grilled
12 slices of tomato, cut in half
8 ounces feta cheese, crumbled into small pieces
1 jar prepared pesto, or freshly made

PESTO
1 bunch fresh basil leaves, stems removed
3 cloves garlic, minced
¼ cup Parmesan cheese
3 tablespoons toasted pine nuts
¼ cup extra virgin olive oil
¼ teaspoon red pepper flakes

Makes 24

1. Place all of the ingredients for the pesto in the bowl of a food processor. Mix until there is a very smooth pesto consistency.
2. Grill the bread on a stove top grill or under the broiler.
3. Drizzle a little olive oil on the bread, place a slice of the tomato on top of the bread. Spoon some of the pesto over the top and sprinkle the feta cheese on top of the pesto. Serve on a large platter.

Corn Bread Tartlets with Ricotta & Green Zebra Tomatoes

1. Preheat the oven to 375 degrees. Butter three 12-cup mini-muffin pans.
2. In a medium bowl, whisk the cornmeal with the flour, sugar, baking powder and salt. In another bowl, whisk the milk with the egg.
3. Pour the milk mixture into the dry ingredients, add the melted butter and stir to combine; do not over mix. Spoon the batter into the muffin cups, filling them halfway.
4. Bake for 10 minutes, or until golden.
5. Transfer the pans to a rack and let cool for about 10 minutes, then turn the muffins out to cool completely.
6. In a medium bowl, toss the tomatoes with the garlic, Parmesan, basil and olive oil and season with salt and pepper. In a small bowl, season the ricotta with salt and pepper and mix well.
7. Using a small knife, slice off the domed tops of the muffins. Top the muffins with the ricotta and the tomatoes and serve.

½ cup stone-ground yellow cornmeal
½ cup all-purpose flour
3 tablespoons sugar
1 teaspoon baking powder
½ teaspoon salt
½ cup milk
1 egg
2 tablespoons unsalted butter, melted
3 Green Zebra or other heirloom tomatoes, halved, seeded and finely chopped
1 garlic clove, minced
1 tablespoon freshly grated Parmesan cheese
1 tablespoon chopped basil
1 tablespoon olive oil
¾ cup whole milk ricotta cheese

Makes 3 Dozen Tartlets

6 ears corn
1 ancho chile, torn into pieces
2 tablespoons corn oil
1 ½ cups chopped onion
1 tablespoon chopped garlic
2 poblano chiles, roasted, peeled,
seeded and chopped
Salt and freshly ground pepper to
taste
½ cup cream

AVOCADO NACHOS
8 ounces cream cheese, softened
2 chipotle chiles in adobo sauce,
chopped
3 tablespoons finely chopped red
onion
2 cloves garlic, finely chopped
1 teaspoon cumin
1 ½ cups grated Monterey Jack
cheese
Salt and freshly ground pepper

½ cup peeled, pitted and finely
diced avocado
2 tablespoons sour cream
1 tablespoon fresh lime juice
1 tablespoon finely chopped
cilantro, plus extra leaves for
garnish
1 tablespoon milk
Salt
6 dozen flat tortilla chips

Serves 6

1. Cut the kernels off the cobs and divide kernels evenly into 2 bowls. Put the cobs in a large saucepan and cover with 2 quarts of water. Add ancho chile pieces. Bring the mixture to a boil over medium-high heat; lower the heat to simmer and cook for 45 minutes. Strain mixture into a bowl; discard cobs and chile pieces.
2. In the same saucepan, heat the corn oil; add onion and garlic and sauté until soft, about 5 minutes. Add one portion of the corn kernels to the onion/garlic mixture and cook until corn is tender, about 10 minutes. Transfer to a blender and add 2 cups of the corn broth. Puree the mixture and strain back into the saucepan.
3. Add the remaining broth, corn and the chiles to the saucepan and cook until corn is tender, another 15 minutes. Salt and pepper to taste. Gently stir in the cream and serve immediately.

AVOCADO NACHOS
1. With an electric mixer, cream together the cream cheese, chipotles, onion, garlic, cumin, Monterey Jack, salt and pepper. Blend well. Cover and refrigerate until ready to use, but bring to room temperature before assembling, so the mixture is spreadable.
2. In a medium bowl, mix together the remaining ingredients and refrigerate, covered, until ready to use. Preheat the broiler. Evenly spread each chip with a generous amount of the cream cheese chipotle mixture. Arrange chips on a baking sheet and broil about 3 minutes away from the heat until puffed and golden. Transfer nachos to a platter and top each with a teaspoon of the avocado cream and a leaf of fresh cilantro.
3. Serve warm.

   NOTE: These nachos are also great if you add 1 cup shredded cooked chicken breast to the cream cheese mixture.

Seared Sea Scallops with Cucumber Red-Pepper Salsa

1. In a large bowl, toss the scallops with the Old Bay Seasoning to coat. Preheat a grill to medium-high heat. Grill the scallops until just cooked in the center, about 3 minutes per side.
2. In a medium bowl, combine all the ingredients for the salsa and stir to blend.
3. Preheat the oven to 350 degrees. Brush the bread with the butter. Sprinkle the cheese evenly over the bread. Dust the cheese with salt and white pepper. Place on a baking sheet and bake until the cheese is melted and golden brown, about 10 minutes. Remove from the oven and transfer to a cutting board. Cut each slice of bread into 4 triangles. Transfer to a wire rack to cool.
4. To serve, place 1 tablespoon salsa on each toast point. Cut the scallops in half horizontally. Place a halved scallop on top of the salsa on each toast point. Drizzle the scallops with the balsamic reduction.

NOTE: Balsamic glaze: In a small heavy sauce pan, bring 1 cup balsamic vinegar to a simmer over medium heat and cook until reduced to syrup. Remove from the heat, let cool, and transfer to a squeeze bottle.

10 large sea scallops
1 tablespoon Old Bay Seasoning

CUCUMBER-RED PEPPER SALSA
1 cucumber, peeled, seeded and finely diced
½ red bell pepper, roasted, peeled and finely diced
1 green onion, chopped
1 tablespoon fresh lemon juice
1 tablespoon chopped fresh cilantro
½ tablespoon chile-garlic paste
Salt and ground white pepper

PEPPERED TOAST POINTS
5 slices firm sandwich bread, such as Pullman bread, crusts removed
2 tablespoons unsalted butter, melted
¼ cup grated Parmesan cheese
Ground white pepper
Balsamic Reduction

Makes 20 Appetizers

Baked Shrimp Saganaki with Feta & Ouzo

1 medium onion, chopped
2 garlic cloves, finely chopped
3 tablespoons olive oil
½ teaspoon red pepper flakes
½ teaspoon ground cinnamon
¼ teaspoon ground allspice
1 (28-ounce) can whole tomatoes in juice, drained,
reserving juice, and chopped
¼ cup ouzo
Pinch of sugar
1 ¼ pounds large peeled and deveined shrimp
⅔ cup feta, crumbled
2 tablespoons chopped mint

Serves 6

This Greek dish is often served as a first course all over Athens and the Greek Islands. It is a delicious combination of heat, spice, creamy feta and fresh mint.

1. Preheat the oven to 375 degrees.
2. Cook onion and garlic in oil with ¼ teaspoon salt in a 4-quart heavy saucepan over medium heat until softened, about 5 minutes. Stir in spices and cook, stirring, 30 seconds. Add chopped tomatoes with juice, ouzo and sugar, and simmer, uncovered, stirring occasionally, until slightly thickened, about 20 minutes. Remove from heat.
3. Season shrimp with ⅛ teaspoon salt, then stir into tomato sauce. Transfer to a 2-quart shallow baking dish and top with feta. Bake until just cooked through, 20 minutes. Serve sprinkled with mint.

Spanish Toast

8 slices sourdough bread
4 garlic cloves, halved
4 small tomatoes, each cut in half crosswise
4 teaspoons olive oil
¼ teaspoon sea salt
¼ teaspoon freshly ground black pepper

Serves 8

1. Prepare the grill.
2. Place bread slices on grill rack; grill 2 minutes on each side or until lightly browned. Rub 1 side of each bread slice with 1 garlic clove half and 1 tomato half (tomato pulp will rub off onto bread. Discard tomato peels.)
3. Drizzle ½ teaspoon olive oil over each bread slice; sprinkle evenly with salt and pepper.

In Barcelona this toast is served with sangria before large platters of paella are brought to the table. Serve the hors d'oeuvre by the pool with pitchers of sangria, Spanish Marcona almonds, Manchego cheese and olives.

Watermelon Margaritas

2 teaspoons sugar
1 lime wedge
3 ½ cups cubed seeded watermelon
½ cup tequila
2 tablespoons sugar
3 tablespoons fresh lime juice
1 tablespoon Triple Sec
Lime wedges and watermelon balls for garnish

Serves 6

1. Place 2 teaspoons sugar in a saucer. Rub the rims of 6 glasses with 1 lime wedge; spin rim of each glass in sugar to coat. Set prepared glasses aside.
2. Combine watermelon, tequila, sugar, lime juice and Triple Sec in a blender; process until smooth.
3. Fill each of the prepared glasses with ½ cup crushed ice. Add ½ cup margarita to each glass. Garnish with lime wedges and melon balls.

MUSTARD SAUCE
1 cup mayonnaise
3 tablespoons Dijon mustard
1 tablespoon Crystal Hot Sauce
3 tablespoons chopped fresh chives, plus extra for garnish
3 tablespoons chopped cilantro
Salt and freshly ground black pepper

1 ball pizza dough
12 favorite hot dogs
1 egg mixed with 1 teaspoon water
Smoked paprika

Serves 12

1. For the sauce, add all of the ingredients in a small bowl
    and stir well to combine. Season with salt and pepper and
    refrigerate until ready to serve.
2. Grill the hot dogs until slightly charred. Set aside to cool.
3. Preheat the oven to 450 degrees. Line the baking sheet
    with parchment paper and spray with nonstick spray.
4. Divide the dough into 12 equal pieces and roll each into a
    long rope about 8 inches long. Wrap each hot dog with 1
    rope, starting at the bottom and twisting it around the hot
    dog until you get to the top. If there is any leftover dough,
    fold it under the hot dog. Brush the egg wash over the
    dough and sprinkle with smoked paprika.
5. Place in the oven and bake until golden brown, 10 to 12
    minutes. Serve on a platter with the mustard sauce and
    garnish with extra chives.

Grilled Chicken Skewers with Sriracha-Honey Crème Frâiche

20 chicken tenders
¼ cup olive oil
Salt and pepper to taste

SRIRACHA-HONEY CREME FRÂICHE
1 cup crème frâiche
2 tablespoons honey
¼ cup chopped scallions
1 tablespoon Sriracha
Salt and pepper

Makes 20

1. Soak 20 wooden skewers in water for 30 minutes. Put the tenders in a shallow bowl and add the olive oil and salt and pepper. Thread the chicken onto the skewers.
2. Preheat a grill until medium hot. Cook the chicken for about 3 minutes on each side until cooked through.
3. Place the crème frâiche, honey, scallions, Sriracha and salt and pepper in a bowl and mix well. Serve the chicken skewers on a platter with the sauce.

Sriracha is made from sun-ripened chiles and is ready to use in soups, pasta, pizza or any dish that you want to add a delicious, spicy taste.

Goat Cheese Gratin

10 ounces soft goat cheese, cubed
2 teaspoons minced fresh rosemary leaves
2 teaspoons minced fresh oregano leaves or a pinch of dried, crushed
1 ½ to 2 cups homemade or your favorite store-bought marinara sauce, at room temperature
About 24 best-quality black olives, pitted

Serves 6

1. Preheat the broiler.
2. Scatter the cheese on the bottom of the baking dish or dishes. Sprinkle with half of the herbs. Spoon on just enough marinara sauce to evenly coat the cheese. Sprinkle with olives and the remaining herbs.
3. Place the baking dish or dishes under the broiler about 3 inches from the heat. Broil until the cheese is melted and fragrant, and the tomato sauce is sizzling, 2 - 3 minutes.

   NOTE: Use six shallow 6-inch round gratin dishes or one 10-inch round baking dish.

This easy hors d'oeuvre was born in Provence. At the end of a week of cooking classes, we always had bits and pieces of goat cheese left. We used them to make this dish.

Garlic Knots

1. Put oven racks in upper and lower thirds of oven and preheat oven to 400 degrees. Lightly oil 2 large baking sheets.
2. Divide dough in half. Keep half of dough covered with a clean kitchen towel. Gently roll out other half into a 10-inch square on a lightly floured surface with a lightly floured rolling pin. If dough is very elastic, cover with a clean towel and let rest about 5 minutes.
3. Cut square in half with a pizza wheel or a sharp heavy knife, then cut each half crosswise into 15 strips. (about ½-inch wide). Cover strips with a clean kitchen towel.
4. Keep remaining strips covered and gently tie each strip into a knot, pulling ends slightly to secure (if dough is sticky, dust lightly with flour.) and arrange knots 1 inch apart in staggered rows on a baking sheet. Keep knots covered with a clean kitchen towel. Repeat with remaining dough on second baking sheet.
5. Bake, switching position of sheets halfway through baking, until golden, 20 to 25 minutes.
6. While knots bake, mince garlic and mash to a paste with salt, then stir together with oil in a very large bowl. Immediately after baking, toss knots in garlic oil, then sprinkle with parsley and cheese and toss to coat. Serve warm or at room temperature.

2 tablespoons olive oil, plus more for the pan
2 pounds pizza dough, thawed completely if frozen
1 garlic clove
¼ teaspoon salt
1 tablespoon finely chopped flat-leaf parsley
½ cup grated Parmesan

Makes 5 Dozen

Pimiento Cheese with Grilled Cornbread

2 cups (8 ounces) grated extra-sharp Cheddar Cheese
2 cups (8 ounces) grated extra-sharp white Cheddar
¼ cup diced piquillo peppers
¼ teaspoon cayenne pepper
½ teaspoon black pepper
⅔ cup mayonnaise

Store bought cornbread, cut into slices
Chopped chives for garnish

Makes About 2 Cups

1. Finely grate cheeses into a large bowl. Stir in the piquillos, cayenne, black pepper, and salt to taste with a fork. Stir in the mayonnaise, mashing mixture with a fork until relatively smooth.
2. Pour the spread into a bowl and chill for about 2 hours.
3. Brush or spray the cornbread slices with olive oil and place on a hot grill until there are nice grill marks. Remove and cool slightly. Spoon a dollop of the pimiento cheese on top and garnish with chopped chives.

Scallop Ceviche Spoons

1 pound sea scallops cut into small pieces
1 cup lime juice
1 cup chopped avocado
½ cup diced red onion
½ cup diced tomato, seeds removed
¼ cup cilantro
2 tablespoons olive oil
2 teaspoons diced jalapeno, seeds removed
½ teaspoon salt
⅛ teaspoon cayenne pepper, plus extra for garnish
¼ easpoon ground cumin

Serves 6

1. Place the scallops and the lime juice in a non-reactive bowl and refrigerate for 3 hours. Remove the seafood from the bowl and reserve the lime juice.
2. Add all of the remaining ingredients to the scallops. Add reserved lime juice to taste. Cover and refrigerate for 1 hour.
3. Mound onto a platter and serve with tortilla or pita chips. Garnish with a sprinkle of cayenne pepper around the edge of the platter and wedges of lime.

   NOTE: For a creative presentation, serve in Chinese soup spoons.

Camerones De Ajo
(Shrimp with Toasted Garlic)

1 cup olive oil
10 cloves garlic, peeled and thinly sliced
1 ½ pounds peeled and deveined shrimp, tail off, split down middle
Salt and freshly ground black pepper
1 lemon
¼ bunch flat leaf parsley, chopped

Serves 6

1. Heat olive oil in a sauté pan over medium-high heat. Add the sliced garlic. Bring to a bare simmer and keep on the lowest heat possible, so the garlic toasts to a golden brown, about 15 minutes.
2. Season shrimp with salt and pepper. Add to the pot and remove from heat. Allow to cook until pink and tender. Finish by squeezing juice of whole lemon over shrimp and sprinkling with chopped parsley. Use a slotted spoon to lift out the prawns and serve on a platter topped with toasted golden garlic shavings and parsley.

This shrimp dish is served in tapas bars all over Spain.

Shrimp Tomatillo Cocktail

1 pound large Tiger prawns, peeled and deveined

SAUCE
8 tomatillos, husked and rinsed
1 red onion, sliced
3 cloves garlic
1 jalapeño pepper
3 tablespoons olive oil
Salt and freshly ground pepper
¼ cup chopped fresh cilantro
1 tablespoon honey

Serves 6 - 8

1. Bring a saucepan of water to a boil. Turn the heat off and put the shrimp in the water for 5 minutes.
2. Do not cover the pan. Remove the shrimp and drain under cold water. To make the sauce, place the tomatillos, onion, garlic and jalapeño in a bowl and toss with the oil, and salt and pepper. Place them on a foil-lined broiler pan and broil until the skin turns black. Place all of the mixture into the bowl of a food processor. Pulse until smooth. Add the cilantro and honey. Season with salt and pepper. If the sauce is too thick, add ½ cup water to thin it a bit. Transfer to a bowl, cover and chill at least 1 hour. Bring to room temperature before serving. Arrange the sauce and shrimp in shot glasses and serve.

Bocconcini Wraps

1 jar roasted red peppers
1 bunch fresh basil leaves
Bocconcini mozzarella balls

Makes 20

Roll thin slices of roasted red pepper around a mini mozzarella ball and place on a basil leaf.

These easy wraps are great to add to an antipasto platter. I've added some caper berries, salami, pro-sciutto and cheese.

Guacamole

2 avocados, pitted, chopped
2 cloves grated garlic
½ cup chopped fresh cilantro
2 tablespoons fresh lime juice
1 jalapeño, finely chopped
1 scallion, finely chopped
Salt to taste

Makes 2 ½ Cups

Pulse the avocados, garlic, cilantro, lime juice and jalapeño in a
food processor until chunky. Add the salt to taste and garnish with
finely chopped scallion.

*In California, guacamole is every
season. We are very lucky that
Haas avocados are locally grown.*

Sangrita in Cucumber Cups

1. Cut two 3 ½ -inch lengths from each of the cucumbers to use as cups. Peel the pieces, leaving a 1 ½ -inch band of peel at one end of each. Using a melon baller, scoop out the seeds, stopping just before reaching the bottom. Refrigerate the cups for at least 10 minutes.
2. Meanwhile, in a small skillet, toast the ancho chile over moderate heat until it begins to blister, about 1 ½ minutes per side. Transfer the ancho to a work surface to cool.
3. In a blender, combine the orange, tomato and lime juices with the onion and Worcestershire sauce; crumble in the toasted ancho and puree. Strain through a coarse sieve. Season the sangrita with salt and pepper and chill for 20 minutes.
4. Pour the sangrita into the cucumber cups and serve.

NOTE: Sangrita is the traditional chaser for shots of tequila.

4 medium cucumbers,
each about 1 ½ inches in diameter
1 dried ancho chile,
stemmed and seeded
1 cup fresh orange juice
1 cup tomato juice
4 tablespoons fresh lime juice
2 tablespoons minced onion
1 teaspoon Worcestershire sauce
Salt and freshly ground pepper

Makes 8 Chasers

The sangrita is delicious to serve for brunch in tall juice glasses too.

Corn Dogs

1. Sift together flour, cornmeal, sugar, baking powder and mustard into a bowl. Whisk together egg, milk and 2 teaspoons oil in another bowl. Add milk mixture to flour mixture, beating with a wooden spoon until batter is smooth.
2. Pour oil into a large, heavy pot to a depth of 3 inches. Heat oil over medium heat to 350 degrees. Meanwhile, dry hot dogs with paper towels, then skewer them with wooden skewers. Dip hot dogs into batter until evenly coated. Gently place battered hot dogs in hot oil and fry, turning once or twice, until crisp and golden, about 3 minutes. Drain on paper towels. Serve with mustard.

1 cup flour
²⁄₃ cup yellow cornmeal
2 tablespoons sugar
1 ½ teaspoons baking powder
¼ teaspoon dry mustard
1 egg, lightly beaten
¾ cup milk
2 teaspoons vegetable oil, plus
vegetable oil for frying
8 hot dogs
8 wooden skewers

Serves 8

AUTUMN

Bloody Mary Shrimp

SHRIMP
1 pound medium shrimp in the shell, peeled and deveined
1 ½ cups thinly sliced celery (3 to 4 ribs)
1 cup thinly sliced scallions (about 6)

SAUCE
½ cup ketchup
¼ cup vodka
¼ cup fresh lemon juice
2 tablespoons bottled horseradish
1 teaspoon Worcestershire sauce
1 teaspoon Tabasco

1 avocado, finely diced
Chinese soup spoons

Makes About 50 Hors D'oeuvres

1. Bring a large saucepan of salted water to a boil. Add shrimp
   and then remove from heat and let stand in water until cooked
   through, about 5 minutes. Drain in a colander and cool to
   room temperature, about 30 minutes. Cut shrimp into thirds
   and transfer to a large bowl with celery and scallions.
2. For the sauce whisk together all of the ingredients, ¼ teaspoon pepper and ¾ teaspoon salt, or to taste.
3. Just before serving, stir sauce into shrimp mixture. Spoon 2
   shrimp pieces with vegetables and sauce into each soup spoon.
   Top with a little chopped avocado. Arrange spoons on a platter.

Fried Polenta with Marinara Sauce

1. Coat an 11x7-inch baking dish with 1 teaspoon of oil. Transfer the hot polenta to the prepared baking dish, spreading evenly to ¾ inch thick. Cover and refrigerate until cold and firm, about 2 hours.
2. Preheat the oven to 250 degrees. Cut the polenta into 2x1-inch pieces. In a large, heavy skillet, heat the remaining ½ cup of oil over a medium-high flame. Working in batches, fry the polenta pieces until golden brown on all sides, about 3 minutes per side. Using tongs, transfer the polenta pieces to paper towels and drain. Place the polenta pieces on a baking sheet and keep warm in the oven while cooking the remaining batches.
3. Transfer the polenta pieces to a serving platter. Sprinkle the polenta with the Parmesan cheese and salt, and serve, passing the marinara sauce on the side.

BASIC POLENTA

In a large, heavy saucepan, bring the water and milk to a boil. Add the salt, then gradually whisk in the cornmeal. Reduce the heat to low and cook, stirring often, until the mixture thickens and the cornmeal is tender, about 15 minutes. Remove from the heat and stir in the butter.

1 teaspoon plus ½ cup olive oil
3 cups basic polenta, freshly made and hot
¼ cup freshly grated Parmesan cheese
2 teaspoons salt
1 cup marinara sauce

BASIC POLENTA
3 cups water
3 cups milk
2 teaspoons salt
1 ¾ cups yellow cornmeal
3 tablespoons unsalted butter, cut into pieces

Makes 30 Pieces

Crispy Shrimp with Chile-Soy Dipping Sauce

1 pound shrimp, shelled and deveined
Shredded filo dough, often called kataifi
Canola oil

CHILE-SOY DIPPING SAUCE
1 tablespoon Chinese hot chile sauce
4 tablespoons soy sauce

Makes 16 Shrimp

1. Wrap each shrimp in some of the shredded filo dough.
2. Heat the canola oil and sauté the shrimp until golden brown.
3. Mix together the Chinese hot chile sauce and soy sauce and serve with the Crispy Shrimp.

   NOTE: Serve the shrimp in a lettuce leaf for presentation.

Double-Cheese Pepperoni Pizza Rolls

2 cups grated Mozzarella cheese (8 ounces)
3 ½ ounces Fontina cheese
3 ½ ounces Pepper Jack cheese
1 package pepperoni
2 teaspoons dried oregano
1 13.8-ounce tube refrigerated pizza dough
Olive oil

Makes 20 Servings

1. Preheat the oven to 425 degrees.
2. Mix the cheeses together with the pepperoni and season with
    salt, pepper and oregano.
3. Unroll dough into rectangle on rimmed baking sheet.
    Mound filling crosswise on lower half of dough, leaving
    1-inch border on the sides. Roll tightly into a log and turn
    the ends under to seal. Bake until puffed and brown, about
    20 minutes. Brush with olive oil. Transfer to a cutting board
    and cut into pieces.

Whole Roasted Garlic with Brie Cheese and Tomatillo-Cilantro Salsa

1. Preheat the oven to 375 degrees.
2. To prepare garlic bulbs: Remove the excess papery skin, but leave the bulbs whole. Cut off the top ½ inch of each bulb, exposing the tops of the individual garlic cloves. Place the garlic bulbs, cut sides up, in a deep-sided casserole or loaf pan and add water to reach halfway up the sides of the bulbs. Drizzle the olive oil evenly over the tops of the bulbs. Cover tightly with foil and place in the oven. Bake until the cloves feel soft when pressed, about 1 hour.
3. Meanwhile, prepare the salsa. Place the tomatillos, onion, garlic and chile under the broiler and char. Add water and vegetables to a blender or food processor. Add the cilantro and whirl until smooth.
4. Do not add the cilantro until just before serving, because it will lose its flavor and color. You will have about ¾ cup salsa.
5. To serve, preheat a broiler. Place 1 piece of the cheese on each of 4 flameproof serving plates. Run the plates under the broiler until the cheese just begins to melt, 3 - 5 minutes. Place a garlic bulb next to the cheese and flood the plate with the salsa.
6. Accompany with French bread or tortillas.

4 whole bulbs garlic
¼ cup olive oil

TOMATILLO-CILANTRO SALSA
⅓ pound tomatillos, husks removed
½ small onion, chopped
1 clove garlic
1 fresh Serrano chile, stemmed
¼ cup water
½ teaspoon salt
½ bunch fresh cilantro
6 ounces Brie cheese, a wheel or cut into 4 equal pieces if serving individually
1 loaf French bread, sliced, or 12 flour tortillas, warmed

Serves 4 - 6

CORN PANCAKES

1 cup all-purpose flour
½ cup yellow cornmeal
2 tablespoons sugar
2 teaspoons baking powder
1 teaspoon salt
½ teaspoon freshly ground black pepper
Pinch of ground red pepper (cayenne)
3 large eggs
¾ cup buttermilk
6 tablespoons unsalted butter, melted
Kernels from 4 ears fresh corn (2 cups fresh or frozen corn)
1 tablespoon chopped fresh basil
1 tablespoon chopped fresh chives
16 tiger prawns

REMOULADE SAUCE

1 cup mayonnaise
¼ cup chopped roasted bell pepper
¼ cup chopped celery
Juice of 1 lemon
1 scallion, trimmed and minced
1 tablespoon chopped fresh parsley
1 tablespoon drained capers
1 teaspoon spicy mustard (Dijon, whole-grain or Cajun)
1 garlic clove, chopped
½ teaspoon hot sauce
¼ teaspoon ground paprika
¼ teaspoon red pepper flakes

Makes 16 hors d'oeuvres

Corn Pancakes with Grilled Tiger Prawns & Remoulade

1. Preheat the oven to 200 degrees.
2. For the pancakes, mix together the flour, cornmeal, sugar, baking powder, salt, black pepper and ground red pepper in a bowl and stir to blend.
3. Combine the eggs, buttermilk, 3 tablespoons of the butter, corn, basil and chives in a separate bowl and stir to mix.
4. Add the flour mixture to the egg mixture and stir until the dry ingredients are moist and blended. Do not over mix.
5. Brush a hot griddle or skillet with the remaining melted butter and heat over medium-high heat. Spoon 1 heaping tablespoon of the mixture onto the griddle or skillet and cook about 2 minutes per side, until the cakes are golden brown and fluffy. This will make 16 small cakes. Place on a baking sheet and keep warm in the oven while you prepare the remaining cakes.
6. For the remoulade place the mayonnaise, roasted red bell pepper, celery, lemon juice, scallion, parsley, capers, mustard, garlic, hot sauce, paprika and red pepper flakes in the bowl of a food processor. Pulse several times until well blended. Do not over mix; this should be chunky.
7. Serve immediately or refrigerate in an airtight container up to 5 days or until ready to use.
8. Toss the cleaned prawns in a bowl with olive oil, salt, pepper and a little paprika. Grill for about 1 minute on each side.
9. To serve, place a corn cake on a plate topped with a prawn and some of the remoulade sauce. Garnish with flat-leaf parsley or scallion greens.

Bruschetta with Roasted Cherry Tomatoes

1 loaf Italian country bread, cut into ¾-inch thick slices
1 cup olive oil, plus additional for drizzling
6 cups cherry tomatoes
2 cloves garlic, finely minced
2 tablespoons capers, drained
2 teaspoons minced basil
2 teaspoons minced fresh oregano
Sea salt

Makes 12 Servings

1. Prepare a grill. Brush the bread with olive oil. Place the bread on the grill until slightly charred. Preheat the oven to 425 degrees.
2. In a large bowl, toss the tomatoes with the garlic, capers, basil and oregano, and ¼ cup olive oil. Spread the tomatoes on a baking sheet in one layer. Roast the tomatoes in the oven for 15 to 20 minutes, until their skins are just starting to split.
3. Spoon the roasted tomatoes and all of their juices on top of the bread slices. Garnish the platter with basil sprigs and sprinkle the bruschetta with a little salt and a little more olive oil. Serve warm.

REMOULADE

¾ cup mayonnaise
¼ cup finely chopped chives
3 teaspoons Dijon mustard
1 teaspoon lemon juice
1 ½ teaspoons garlic,
finely chopped
¼ teaspoon cayenne, or to taste
Salt and freshly ground pepper

Combine the mayonnaise, chives, mustard, , lemon juice, garlic and cayenne pepper. Add salt and pepper to taste. Spoon topping onto crab cakes. Serve at room temperature.

Shrimp Beignets with Spicy Remoulade Sauce

1. Heat the oil in a skillet over medium-high heat. Add the onions. Season with salt and cayenne. Sauté for about 2 minutes, or until slightly wilted. Add the peppers and garlic and continue to sauté for 1 minute. Season the shrimp with Creole seasoning. Add the shrimp to the pan and sauté for 2 minutes. Stir in ¼ cup of the green onions. Remove and set aside to cool.

2. Combine the beaten eggs, milk and baking powder. Season with salt and pepper. Add the flour, ¼ cup at a time, beating and incorporating until all is used and the batter is smooth. This can be done in a blender. Remove and add the seafood mixture to the batter and fold to mix. Season with salt and cayenne, Worcestershire sauce and hot sauce. Heat the oil to 360 degrees.

3. Drop the batter, a heaping tablespoon at a time, into the hot oil. When the beignets pop to the surface, roll them around with a slotted spoon in the oil to brown them evenly. Remove and drain on paper towels. Season with a little of the Creole seasoning and serve with the remoulade sauce.

The beignets can be made ahead and re-heated before serving.

SHRIMP BEIGNETS
1 tablespoon canola oil
½ cup chopped onions
Salt
Cayenne pepper
¼ cup minced red pepper
¼ cup minced yellow pepper
2 tablespoons chopped garlic
1 pound medium shrimp, peeled, deveined and roughly chopped
½ cup chopped green onions
3 eggs, beaten
1 ½ cups milk
2 teaspoons baking powder
3 ¼ cups flour
Dash of Worcestershire sauce
Dash of hot sauce
Pinch of Creole seasoning
Vegetable oil for frying

Makes 2 Dozen

Red-Chile Deviled Egg Salad on Taco Chips

8 large eggs
¼ cup mayonnaise
2 teaspoons chipotle chile puree
2 teaspoons ancho chile powder, plus extra for garnish
2 tablespoons chopped chives
2 tablespoons finely chopped fresh cilantro
Salt and freshly ground black pepper

Serves 8

1. Put the eggs in a medium saucepan and add enough cold water to cover them by 1 inch. Bring just to a boil over high heat and then turn heat down and simmer for 8 minutes. Drain the eggs and run under cold water to cool. Remove the shell from each egg.
2. Slice each egg in half lengthwise and carefully remove the yolk. Place the yolks in a medium bowl and mash with a fork. Add the mayonnaise, chipotle puree, ancho powder, chives and cilantro and stir until combined; season with salt and pepper.
3. For deviled eggs, carefully spoon the mixture back into the egg whites. For Deviled Egg Salad, chop the egg whites and combine with the yolk mixture. This can be made up to 8 hours in advance. To serve, spoon onto a taco chip with a leafy green and dust with ancho powder.

   NOTE: For a heavier hors d'oeuvre add crab, shrimp or salmon to the yolk mixture. I have also added cooked bacon.

Spinach Soufflé-Stuffed Mushrooms

1 package frozen chopped spinach, thawed and squeezed dry
½ pound Havarti cheese, cut into ½ -inch cubes
⅓ cup grated Parmesan cheese
3 eggs
2 tablespoons milk
1 teaspoon finely chopped garlic
1 teaspoon dried oregano
½ teaspoon black pepper
½ teaspoon ground nutmeg
2 pounds medium-size white mushrooms (about 30), stems removed and caps cleaned

Makes About 2 ½ Dozen

1. Heat the oven to 375 degrees.
2. Remove stems from mushrooms. Place mushrooms on baking sheet and bake for 10 minutes. Drain liquid. Put the spinach, Havarti, Parmesan, eggs, milk, garlic, oregano, pepper and nutmeg in a food processor. Pulse until cheese is finely chopped.
3. Coat mushrooms with cooking spray; sprinkle with salt. Fill each cap with 1 level tablespoon spinach mixture.
4. Bake for 25 minutes or until mushrooms are tender and the filling is set.

Grilled Chile-Cheese Toasts

1 pound whole milk mozzarella, shredded
½ cup finely chopped onion
1 medium tomato, finely chopped and drained on paper towels
2 jalapenos, seeded and finely chopped
½ cup chopped cilantro
½ cup mayonnaise
½ teaspoon cayenne pepper
Salt and freshly ground black pepper
Twelve ½-inch-thick slices Tuscan bread

Serves 6

1. Preheat the grill. In a large bowl, mix together all of the ingredients except the bread.
2. Arrange bread slices on grill. Grill on both sides. Let cool slightly, then spread with mozzarella cheese mixture on top. Place under the broiler for 3 to 5 minutes, until melted and slightly browned. Serve hot.

Blue Cheese Popovers

2 large eggs
1 cup milk
2 tablespoons butter, melted, plus more for tins
1 cup all-purpose flour
½ teaspoon salt
⅛ teaspoon freshly ground black pepper
1 ¼ ounces blue cheese, crumbled
1 tablespoon roughly chopped fresh thyme

Makes 4 Dozen

1. In a blender, mix the eggs, milk, melted butter, flour, salt and pepper. Blend until all of the lumps have disappeared. Whisk in the cheese and the thyme. Transfer the batter to an airtight container. The batter must be very cold before using; refrigerate for at least 2 hours or overnight.
2. Preheat the oven to 425 degrees. Generously butter the mini muffin tins. Preheat muffin tins until very hot.
3. Fill each cup to the top with the chilled batter. Bake the popovers until golden and puffed, about 20 minutes. Repeat until all the batter is used. Serve warm.

CRAB SPRING ROLLS

1 skein (about 2 ounces) bean thread noodles, if not
available use angel hair pasta
1 tablespoon vegetable oil
⅓ cup finely chopped shallots
1 garlic clove, crushed
1 medium carrot, peeled and cut
into 2-inch long matchsticks
8 ounces crabmeat, flaked and picked over
1 cup coarsely chopped bean sprouts
¼ cup chopped fresh cilantro
2 tablespoons Asian fish sauce
1 teaspoon sugar
¼ teaspoon hot chili sauce or Tabasco sauce

15 egg roll wrappers
Canola oil for deep-frying

SWEET GARLIC SAUCE
½ cup rice vinegar
½ cup sugar
¼ cup water
3 garlic cloves, thinly sliced
½ teaspoon Chinese chili paste
with garlic

Makes 15 Spring Rolls

Crab Spring Rolls

1. In a small saucepan, mix the vinegar, sugar, water, garlic and chili paste together. Bring to a simmer over medium heat, stirring to dissolve the sugar. Remove from heat and let stand until cool. The sauce can be prepared up to 1 day ahead and stored at room temperature.
2. In a medium bowl, cover the noodles with very hot water. Let stand until the noodles are soft and supple, about 10 minutes. Drain well in a sieve. Using kitchen scissors, snip through the bean threads in the sieve to cut them into more manageable lengths. Place in a bowl, cover with plastic wrap, and set aside.
3. Heat a large skillet over high heat. Add the oil and tilt to coat the inside of the pan. Add the shallots and garlic and stir-fry, until fragrant, about 15 seconds. Add the carrot and stir-fry until crisp tender, about 1 minutes. Add the crab, bean sprouts, cilantro, fish sauce, sugar , and chili or Tabasco sauce and stir fry until heated through, about 2 minutes. Remove from the heat and place in a shallow dish. Stir in the bean threads. Let cool completely.
4. Preheat the oven to 200 degrees. Line a baking sheet with parchment paper. Place an egg roll wrapper on a work surface, with the points at 12, 3, 6 and 9 o'clock. Place about ¼ cup filling on the bottom third of the wrapper and form it into a log that comes no closer than ½ inch to the edges of the wrapper. Fold up the bottom point and roll up the egg roll, folding in the side points as you roll it into a tight cylinder. Place a dab of water on the last point to adhere it to the roll. Place the spring roll, seam-side down on the parchment paper. Repeat with the remaining filling and wrappers.
5. Place a large wire cake rack over a jelly roll pan. In a deep Dutch oven, add vegetable shortening to a depth of 2 to 3 inches and heat over high heat to 365 degrees. In batches, without crowding, deep fry the spring rolls until golden brown, about 3 minutes. Using a wire-mesh skimmer, transfer to the wire rack and keep warm in the oven while deep frying the remaining spring rolls. Serve immediately, with small bowls of the garlic sauce for dipping.

NOTE: May also serve with hot mustard and plum sauce.

Sangria

1 lemon
1 lime
1 orange
1 ½ cups rum
½ cup sugar
1 bottle dry red wine
1 cup fresh orange juice

Serves 6

1. Chill the fruit, rum, wine and orange juice. Slice the lemon, lime and orange into thin rounds. Put in a tall pitcher. Pour in the rum and sugar. Chill for 2 hours.
2. When ready to serve, crush the fruit lightly with a wooden spoon. Stir in the wine and orange juice and stir.
3. Serve in chilled wine glasses.

Shrimp Toast Puffs with Soy-Garlic Sauce

1. Preheat the oven to 425 degrees.
2. Place the shrimp in a food processor; pulse until finely chopped. Cook bacon in a large nonstick skillet over medium-high heat until crisp. Remove bacon from pan, reserving 2 teaspoons drippings in pan. Add shrimp to reserved drippings in pan, and sauté 3 minutes. Add ⅓ cup green onions to pan; sauté 1 minute. Stir in ginger.
3. Lightly spoon flour into a dry measuring cup; level with a knife. Combine 1 cup water, butter and sugar in a large heavy saucepan; bring to a boil, stirring occasionally with a wooden spoon. Reduce heat to low; add flour, stirring well until mixture is smooth and pulls away from sides of pan. Remove from heat. Add egg whites and egg, 1 at a time; beat with a mixer at medium speed until smooth. Gently stir in shrimp mixture.
4. Drop dough by level tablespoons, 2 inches apart, onto baking sheets coated with cooking spray. Bake for 10 minutes. Reduce oven temperature to 350 and bake an additional 10 minutes or until browned and crisp.
5. Combine soy sauce and remaining ingredients in a small bowl, stirring with a whisk.

PUFFS
1 pound peeled and deveined medium shrimp
2 bacon slices, diced
⅓ cup finely chopped green onions
1 ½ teaspoons bottled ground fresh ginger (such as Spice World)
1 cup all-purpose flour
1 cup water
3 tablespoons butter
½ teaspoon sugar
2 large egg whites
1 large egg
Cooking spray

SOY-GARLIC SAUCE
¼ cup soy sauce
2 tablespoons finely chopped green onions
2 tablespoons seasoned rice vinegar
1 teaspoon hot chili sauce with garlic
½ teaspoon dark sesame oil

Serves 8

Bruschetta with Braised Cannellini Beans, Arugula and Pecorino

4 cans cannellini beans, drained and rinsed
3 cloves garlic, thinly sliced
1 teaspoon chopped marjoram
1 teaspoon chopped oregano
¾ cup chicken stock
3 tablespoons olive oil
Ciabatta, cut into slices and grilled with olive oil
2 cups arugula
Block of pecorino for shaving
Olive oil

Serves 6

1. Heat 3 tablespoons olive oil in a skillet and sauté the garlic. Add the cannellini beans, fresh herbs and chicken stock. Bring to a simmer just to heat through, and then remove from the heat.
2. Spoon about ⅓ cup of the beans onto the grilled bruschetta , and top with a small handful of arugula.
3. Using a vegetable peeler, shave a few curls of pecorino on top, and finish with a drizzle of olive oil. Serve immediately.

Crab and Eggplant Stacks with Herb Oil and Sun-Dried Tomato Crust

1. Combine all the ingredients for the herb oil in a blender and puree until smooth.
2. Pour half of the herb oil into a large baking dish and add the eggplant slices. Let stand at room temperature for 15 minutes, turning the slices halfway through. Remove from the marinade and shake off the excess.
3. Combine the sun-dried tomato crust ingredients in a food processor and pulse until finely ground. Set aside. In a large bowl, combine the filling ingredients; stir to blend and set aside.
4. Preheat the oven to 400 degrees.
5. In a large sauté pan or skillet, heat ¼ inch oil over medium-high heat until shimmering. Dredge the eggplant slices in the flour, shaking off the excess.
6. Add to the pan and sauté until golden brown, about 5 minutes on each side. Using a slotted metal spatula, transfer to paper towels to drain.
7. Repeat with the remaining slices. Put 6 eggplant slices on a baking sheet and spread each slice with ¼ cup of the crab filling.
8. Top with the remaining eggplant slices. Spread about ¼ cup of the sun-dried tomato mixture on each top slice.
9. Bake for 15 to 20 minutes or until the crusts are browned and the filling is hot.
10. To serve, place the stacks on a platter and drizzle with some of the remaining herb oil and the balsamic glaze.

NOTE: Balsamic glaze: In a small heavy saucepan, bring 1 cup balsamic vinegar to a simmer over medium heat and cook until reduced to syrup. Remove from the heat, let cool, and transfer to a squeeze bottle.

HERB OIL
1 cup olive oil
¼ cup whole basil leaves
¼ cup flat-leaf parsley, chopped
1 teaspoon fresh lemon juice
1 teaspoon salt
½ teaspoon freshly ground pepper

12 ¼ inch thick eggplant slices

SUN-DRIED TOMATO CRUST
2 cups fresh bread crumbs
½ cup julienned oil packed sun-dried tomatoes
2 tablespoons minced fresh basil
1 teaspoon salt
½ teaspoon freshly ground pepper
¼ teaspoon red pepper flakes

CRAB FILLING
1 pound lump crab meat
1 tablespoon finely diced red pepper
1 teaspoon Dijon mustard
1 cup mayonnaise
½ cup fresh bread crumbs

Olive oil for sautéing
Flour for dredging
Balsamic glaze

Serves 6

Caramelized Pear Crostini with Prosciutto and Goat Cheese

1. Heat the butter and olive oil in a large skillet over medium-high heat until the butter is sizzling. Place the pear slices in the skillet and cook for about 1 minute, until they begin to brown. Add the vinegar and sprinkle the sugar on top.
2. Bring to a boil, shaking the pan and cook until the liquid reduces to a sticky syrup, about 2 minutes. Sprinkle with salt and pepper to taste and set aside to cool slightly.
3. In a small bowl, combine the goat cheese and parsley. Spread each crostini with about 1 tablespoon of the goat cheese and top with a slice of prosciutto and a slice of pear.

1 tablespoon unsalted butter
Splash of olive oil
4 Bartlett pears cut into 24 slices
2 tablespoons balsamic vinegar
1 tablespoon sugar
Salt and freshly ground black pepper
6 ounces goat cheese, at room temperature
2 tablespoons chopped fresh parsley
24 crostini (slice a baguette into ¼-inch slices and toast)
24 thin slices prosciutto'

Makes 2 Dozen

Hummus

4 cups (2 ½ cans) garbanzos, drained
¼ cup tahini (sesame paste)
⅓ cup warm water, chicken stock or vegetable stock
2 tablespoons olive oil
Juice of 2 lemons
3 - 4 garlic cloves
1 ½ teaspoons salt
2 teaspoons ground cumin seed
Pinch cayenne
2 tablespoons chopped parsley

Yields 1 Quart

1. Combine garbanzos, tahini, warm water, olive oil and juice of 1 lemon in the bowl of a food processor. Process until smooth and creamy.
2. Add garlic, salt, cumin seed, cayenne and parsley and process to blend. Taste and correct seasoning if necessary.
3. Add more lemon juice to taste.
4. Put into a container, cover and refrigerate until ready to use.
5. Serve this Middle-Eastern garbanzos and sesame spread as a dip with hot pita bread or as a component of a cold lunch or appetizer plate.

Grilling the pita bread adds a smoky flavor to the hummus.

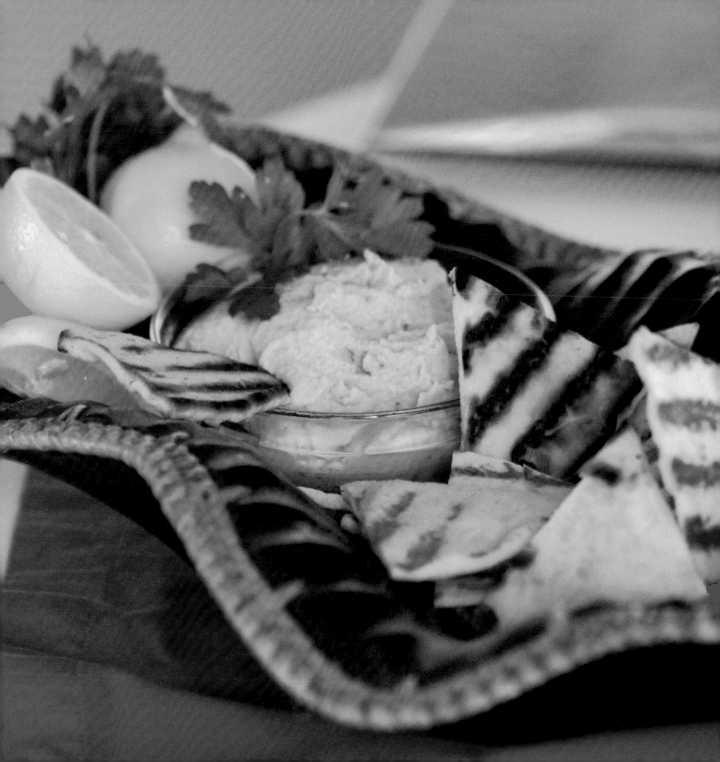

Lettuce Wraps with Spicy Pork

1. Preheat an oven to 350 degrees.
2. In a small bowl, combine the Chinese five spice, salt and pepper. Rub the mixture evenly on the pork. In a Dutch oven warm 2 tablespoons of the oil. Brown the pork on all sides. Transfer to a large bowl.
3. Reduce the heat to medium and warm the remaining 1 tablespoon of oil. Add the onion and cook, stirring occasionally, until softened, about 5 minutes. Add the ginger and garlic and cook, stirring frequently, for 1 minute. Add the soy sauce, the hoisin sauce, chili sauce and the broth and bring to a simmer. Return the pork to the pot. Cover the pot, transfer to the oven and bake until it is fork tender, about 2 ½ to 3 hours.
4. Skim the fat off the sauce. Using tongs and a fork, pull the pork apart into chunks.
5. Serve in the lettuce leaves with green onions and cilantro. Pass extra hoisin sauce and chili sauce.

NOTE: If using vacuum packed pork , sauté the onion and other ingredients and add the pork to it.

It is possible to buy already cooked pork now in vacuum packages, they finish cooking in the microwave in about 6 minutes. Save about 3 hours.

5 pounds boneless pork shoulder, cut into large pieces*
2 teaspoons Chinese five spice powder
1 teaspoon salt
3 tablespoons canola oil
1 onion, diced
1 ½ tablespoons grated fresh ginger
1 tablespoon minced garlic
½ cup soy sauce
⅓ cup hoisin sauce
2 tablespoons Sriracha chili sauce
1 ½ cups chicken broth
Butter lettuce leaves
Thinly sliced green onions

Serves 12

Brioche Crab Melts

8 small round brioche dinner rolls, or one loaf of brioche sliced
6 tablespoons truffle butter or unsalted butter, softened
½ cup mayonnaise
¼ cup minced red onion
¼ cup chopped flat-leaf parsley
1 tablespoon fresh lime juice
½ Granny Smith apple, quartered lengthwise, cored and thinly sliced crosswise
Several dashes of hot sauce
Salt and freshly ground pepper
1 pound lump crabmeat
1 ½ cups shredded Gruyere cheese

Serves 8

1. Preheat the broiler. Spread the cut sides of the brioche with the truffle butter and set on a baking sheet, cut sides up. Broil the rolls 6 inches from the heat, until toasted. Reduce the oven temperature to 400 degrees.
2. In a large bowl, mix the mayonnaise, red onion, parsley, lime juice, apple and hot sauce and season with salt and pepper. Fold in the crabmeat.
3. Set the top halves of the rolls aside. Top the bottoms with the crab salad and sprinkle with the Gruyere. Bake in the upper third of the oven until the cheese is melted. Close the crab melts or serve open-faced.

Turkey Meatball Parmigiana Sliders

2 dozen fresh or frozen pre-made turkey meatballs
Marinara sauce, home-made or your favorite store-bought
2 dozen rolls, split
1 ½ cups grated mozzarella cheese
½ cup finely grated Parmesan
Basil leaves

Makes 2 Dozen

1. Place the meatballs into the marinara sauce and bring to a simmer. Season the marinara to taste. Preheat the oven to 400 degrees.
2. Arrange the rolls, cut side up on a baking sheet. Place 1 meatball, a spoonful of sauce, 1 tablespoon mozzarella and 1 teaspoon Parmesan on bottom halves. Bake until cheese melts, about 3 minutes. Sandwich with a basil leaf.
3. Serve on a large tray with additional basil.

WINTER

Mozzarella Grilled Roman-Style

1. Cut the bread and the mozzarella into ½ -inch-thick slices. You will need 20 slices of bread and 16 slices of mozzarella.
2. Preheat the broiler.
3. Thread the bread and cheese onto skewers, starting with the bread and alternating with the cheese. Press the end slices toward the center so that everything is closely packed together. Place the skewers on an oiled baking sheet. Brush the slices of bread and cheese with 2 tablespoons of the oil and season them with salt and pepper. Put the baking sheet on the middle shelf of the preheated broiler, 5 or 6 inches from the flame. Broil for about 7-10 minutes, checking to make sure the bread does not burn.
4. Meanwhile, heat the butter and the remaining tablespoon of oil in a heavy saucepan over low heat. When the butter is completely melted, remove the pan from the heat. Add the garlic. Taste for salt and pepper.
5. Remove the skewers from the broiler, place each on an individual plate and pour some of the sauce over each serving. Garnish with a sprig of parsley and chopped rosemary.

1 thin loaf Italian bread
3 medium-sized mozzarella (about 1 ½ pounds total weight)
3 tablespoons olive oil
Salt and freshly ground black pepper
8 tablespoons butter
4 cloves garlic, grated

GARNISH
Sprigs of Italian parsley
1 teaspoon chopped rosemary

Serves 6

Mini Beef Filets with Horseradish Cream on Crostini

2 pounds beef filet, center cut, trimmed
2 tablespoons olive oil
2 tablespoons crushed black pepper
Salt
½ cup crème frâiche
2 tablespoons horseradish, drained
1 tablespoon chopped fresh thyme
48 crostini

GARNISH
3 large sprigs fresh thyme

Makes 48 Crostini

1. Cut the beef lengthwise into 4 equal pieces to form 4 mini filets. Brush the entire surface of each filet with olive oil, and rub ½ tablespoon of black pepper into each mini filet. Season to taste with salt.
2. Heat 1 tablespoon of olive oil in a large skillet over high heat. When the oil is hot, add 1 or 2 filets and sear, turning frequently, until the outside is brown and the center is still rare, 3 to 4 minutes. Remove from the skillet and set aside to cool. Repeat with the remaining filets.
3. Mix together the crème frâiche, horseradish and chopped thyme in a bowl. Season to taste with salt and pepper.
4. When the filets have cooled, slice each into ½-inch-thick slices, place on the crostini, and top with a little horseradish-crème frâiche. Garnish each with a small sprig of thyme

Hot Crab Dip with Toasts

1. Preheat the oven to 400 degrees.
2. Melt 2 tablespoons of the butter in a medium saucepan over medium heat. Add the shallots and cook until soft, about 2 minutes. Add 1 tablespoon of water and simmer for 30 seconds. Stir in the cayenne, Old Bay, and dry mustard until well mixed. Pour the half and half into the saucepan and bring to a simmer. Slowly whisk in the cream cheese, a few pieces at a time. When the cream cheese is fully incorporated, whisk in the Cheddar cheese a bit at a time. Stir for 2 to 3 minutes. Remove from the heat.
3. Add the lemon juice and Worcestershire and stir. Add the crab meat and half of the parsley and stir.
4. Transfer the mixture to an ovenproof baking dish and sprinkle with the bread pieces. Dot the top of the bread pieces with the remaining tablespoon of butter. Sprinkle with the paprika.
5. Bake for 20 minutes., until the bread pieces are golden and the dip is hot. Garnish with the remaining parsley and serve with toast points.

TOAST POINTS:
12 thin slices white sandwich bread, crusts removed. Cut each bread slice in half on the diagonal. Heat the oven to 300 degrees. Arrange the triangles on a baking sheet. Bake, turning once, until the triangles are dry and slightly toasted, 5 minutes per side. Transfer to a wire rack to cool. Store in an airtight container.

3 tablespoons butter
2 medium shallots, minced
¼ teaspoon cayenne pepper
¾ teaspoon Old Bay seasoning
1 ½ teaspoons dry mustard
¾ cup half and half
8 ounces cream cheese, cut into small pieces
4 ounces sharp white Cheddar cheese, grated on the large holes of a box grater (1 ¾ cups)
3 tablespoons fresh lemon juice
2 teaspoons Worcestershire sauce
10 ounces lump crab meat, picked over
½ cup chopped Italian parsley
2 slices white bread, crusts removed, torn into ¼-inch pieces
½ teaspoon paprika

Makes About 3 Cups

I sometimes add spinach and artichoke hearts for a heartier dip.

Cheese Straws

1. Mix the cheese, salt and cayenne pepper together in a small bowl.
2. Dust the work surface with flour. If the pastry dough is packed in two ½-pound sheets, roll one sheet of pastry to a 10x8 inch rectangle. Brush the entire surface of the dough with the beaten egg and sprinkle 1 cup of the cheese mixture over the top half of the dough. Fold the bottom half of the dough over the cheese and press the edges with the rolling pin to seal, then press the dough gently in a few places to make the layers stick together. Roll the dough into a 10x8 inch rectangle. Sprinkle ¼ cup of the cheese mixture over the top of the dough, and with a rolling pin press the cheese into the dough.
3. Using a pizza wheel, trim the edges of the dough and cut it into ¾-inch-wide strips. Twist the strips loosely 4 or 5 times from the center out, and place them on a parchment lined cookie sheet. Repeat this procedure with the second sheet of pastry. Place the cookie sheets in the refrigerator to allow the pastry dough to rest for 30 minutes.
4. Preheat the oven to 400 degrees.
5. Bake the cheese straws for 12 to 15 minutes until golden. Remove them from the oven and cool on a wire rack. Serve at room temperature.

NOTE: Cheese straws are best the day that they are made but keep for several days in a tightly sealed container. Arrange them in a rustic basket or crystal glass container and serve with cocktails.

1 ½ cups finely grated Parmesan cheese
1 cup finely grated sharp Cheddar cheese
½ teaspoon salt
¼ to ½ teaspoon cayenne pepper
Flour for dusting work surface
1 pound frozen puff pastry, defrosted
1 egg, beaten

Makes About 48 Straws

Blue Cheese, Walnut and Cranberry Crostini

24 ¼-inch thick slices ciabatta bread
2 tablespoons walnut oil
½ cup chopped toasted walnuts
8 ounces blue cheese, crumbled
4 tablespoons shallots, chopped
1/3 cup dried cranberries
Micro greens
2 tablespoons shallots, chopped
2 tablespoons walnut oil
1 tablespoon sherry vinegar
Sea salt

Makes 24

1. Preheat the oven to 400 degrees. Arrange bread slices on
    baking sheet. Brush bread slices on top side with 2 table-
    spoons walnut oil. Bake until crisp, about 5 minutes.
2. Mix walnuts, cheese, 4 tablespoons shallots and dried cranber-
    ries in a medium bowl. Spread mixture on toasts. Bake until
    cheese melts, about 4 minutes.
3. Mix the micro greens, 2 tablespoons shallots, 2 tablespoons
    walnut oil and vinegar in a bowl. Sprinkle with sea salt; toss.
    Serve on the crostini.

Crab Cake Sliders with Remoulade Sauce

1. For the crab cakes mix thoroughly together the mayonnaise, egg white, lemon juice, dry mustard, Old Bay Seasoning, cayenne, salt and pepper. Fold the crab meat into the mixture with a spatula. Add the dry bread crumbs.
2. Prepare fresh bread crumbs by removing the crust from 6-8 pieces of regular white bread and processing in a food processor for approximately one minute. Mix the bread crumbs into crab mixture. Form into cakes and refrigerate for 30 minutes.
3. Preheat the oven to 400 degrees. Roll the crab cakes in additional fresh bread crumbs and place on a baking sheet. Spray with olive oil spray. Bake for 20 minutes until crispy on the outside.
4. Make the remoulade sauce by combining all of the ingredients together in a small bowl.
5. Grill the hamburger buns. Top with a piece of the butter lettuce, followed by a crab cake, remoulade sauce, heirloom tomato and a slice of red onion. Put the hamburger top on and secure with a long toothpick.
6. Serve on a large platter.

NOTE: Freeze any leftover bread crumbs for use another time.

CRAB CAKES
1 cup mayonnaise
1 egg white
3 tablespoons lemon juice
2 teaspoons dry mustard
2 teaspoons Old Bay Seasoning
½ teaspoon cayenne
Pinch salt and pepper
1 pound lump crab meat
½ cup fine, dried bread crumbs
2 cups fresh bread crumbs, plus extra for coating

REMOULADE SAUCE
¾ cup mayonnaise
¼ cup finely chopped chives
3 teaspoons Dijon mustard
1 ½ teaspoons garlic, grated
¼ teaspoon cayenne, or to taste
Salt and freshly ground black pepper

Mini hamburger buns
Heirloom tomato slices
Butter lettuce
Thinly sliced red onion

Serves 12

Beef Tenderloin Yakitori

24 bamboo skewers
¼ cup soy sauce, divided
¼ cup mirin, divided
2 tablespoons sake, divided
1 pound beef tenderloin, trimmed and cut into cubes
2 tablespoons sugar
1 bunch green onions cut into 1-inch pieces
1 teaspoon sesame oil

Makes 2 Dozen

1. Soak skewers in water at least 30 minutes.
2. Combine 1 tablespoon each soy sauce, mirin and sake in a medium bowl. Add beef, tossing to coat. Let stand at least 30 minutes.
3. Combine remaining 3 tablespoons each soy sauce and mirin, remaining 1 tablespoon sake and sugar in a small saucepan over medium-high heat. Simmer 5 to 8 minutes or until glaze is slightly syrupy. Set aside.
4. Combine green onions and sesame oil; toss well. Thread green onion pieces and beef alternately onto skewers. Cover and chill until ready to grill.
5. Grill skewers over medium-high heat for 1 minute. Turn skewers over; brush with glaze and grill 2 minutes more or until desired degree of doneness.

Queso Fundido with Chorizo

1. Char chiles under the broiler until blackened on all sides; place in a plastic bag for 10 minutes. Peel, seed, and coarsely chop chiles.
2. Sauté the chorizo and garlic in a large cast-iron skillet over medium-high heat until browned for about 10 minutes. Add the green onion; stir until wilted, about 5 minutes. Remove from the heat. Mix in the cilantro and poblano chiles.
3. Toss both cheeses and cornstarch in a large bowl until coated. Bring 2 cups chicken broth to a simmer in a large pot over medium-high heat. Add cheese by cupfuls, whisking until each addition is almost melted before adding the next. Remove from the heat. Stir in chorizo mixture. Thin with more broth if it is too thick. Season with salt and pepper.
4. Serve in the cast-iron skillet with tortilla chips.

5 large poblano chiles
1 ¼ pounds soy chorizo
5 large garlic cloves, chopped
24 green onions, chopped
2 ½ cups chopped fresh cilantro
1 ¼ pounds Monterey Jack cheese, coarsely grated (about 5 cups)
1 ¼ pounds whole-milk mozzarella cheese, coarsely grated (about 5 cups)
2 ½ tablespoons cornstarch
2 cups chicken broth

Tortilla chips

Serves 20

Antipasto Platter

This platter is great to do for a crowd. Everyone can help themselves to what they like. Colorful and delicious.

For an interesting plate of hors d'oeuvres choose an assortment from the following:

Bruschetta
Caponata
Marinated Artichokes
Bocconcini
Goat cheese marinated in herbs or in pesto vinaigrette
Roasted red peppers
Buffalo Mozzarella, tomatoes and basil
Grilled eggplant
Zucchini slices
Fontina cheese
Assorted salamis
Mortadella
Marinated olives

Cornmeal-Coated Chiles Rellenos with Spicy Black Bean Sauce

1. In a mixing bowl, combine the beer, eggs, milk, flour and melted butter and mix well. Add salt and pepper to taste and set aside.
2. Mix together the cheeses and stuff the peppers with them. Batter lightly and dredge in cornmeal. In a large frying pan over high heat, heat the oil to 375 degrees, or until a drop of batter sizzles. Fry the peppers, turning until lightly browned, about 4 minutes. Drain briefly on paper towels. Serve hot. May be made the same day and refrigerated, covered. Reheat in a 350 degree oven just before serving.
3. Spoon a layer of black bean sauce on a plate and place a chile on top of the sauce. Garnish with chopped chives, tomatoes, and a sprig of cilantro.

BLACK BEAN SAUCE

1. In a large saucepan over medium heat, heat the oil and sweat the onion, garlic, and jalapeno. Add the wine, raise the heat and reduce until the liquid is almost completely evaporated. Add the beans and stock, reduce the heat and simmer for 30 minutes.
2. Add the cumin and salt and pepper to taste. Place in a food processor and process to a smooth puree. May be refrigerated, covered, for up to 2 days. Before serving, bring to room temperature.

An hors d'oeuvre to share with friends or a first course. I had this years ago at Bobby Flay's Mesa Grill.

BEER BATTER

1 ½ cups beer (Tecate)
2 large eggs, lightly beaten
½ cup milk
2 ½ cups all-purpose flour
2 tablespoons melted butter
Salt and freshly ground pepper

8 tablespoons crumbled goat cheese
8 tablespoons grated Monterey Jack
8 Poblano peppers, roasted, seeded and peeled
4 cups yellow cornmeal
3 cups canola oil
Spicy Black Bean Sauce
Chives, chopped tomato and cilantro for garnish

SPICY BLACK BEAN SAUCE

2 tablespoons oil
1 medium onion, coarsely chopped
2 garlic cloves, minced
1 jalapeno, minced
½ cup white wine
3 cups cooked or canned black beans, drained
2 cups chicken stock
2 tablespoons cumin

Serves 8

Pumpernickel with Smoked Salmon & Horseradish Crème Frâiche

¾ cup crème frâiche
½ cup finely chopped red onion
1 tablespoon finely chopped dill, plus
24 tiny sprigs for garnish
2 teaspoons prepared horseradish
Salt and freshly ground pepper
Twenty-four 3-inch triangle or square-shaped slices, cut from ¾ pound
loaf of pumpernickel.
½ pound thickly sliced smoked salmon
2 ounces caviar, optional

Makes 24

1. In a small bowl, combine the crème frâiche, onion, chopped
   dill and horseradish. Stir well and season with salt and pepper.
2. Cover each bread triangle with smoked salmon, trimming it
   to fit. Top each triangle with 2 teaspoons of the sauce, a little
   caviar and a dill sprig.

Tapenade

13 ounces black Mediterranean-style olives
4 anchovy fillets
⅓ cup drained capers
⅓ cup olive oil
2 cloves garlic, peeled and minced
1 tablespoon lemon juice
Black pepper

Serves 6

1. Pit the olives and place in a food processor.
2. Add the anchovy fillets, capers, oil and garlic.
3. Turn machine on and off to chop the ingredients to a grainy texture.
4. Add the lemon juice, pepper and blend. Taste and add more olive oil, lemon juice or pepper if needed.
5. Pack the tapenade in a crock jar to serve or spread on crisp French bread toasts.

Salmon Tartare on Potato Crisps

1 8-inch long russet potato
2 tablespoons canola oil
Salt and freshly ground black pepper
1 pound skinless, boneless salmon filet
3 tablespoons Dijon mustard
2 tablespoons chopped cornichons
2 tablespoons chopped red onions
2 tablespoons capers
2 tablespoons olive oil
2 tablespoons finely chopped parsley
1 tablespoon finely chopped chives

Serves 8

1. Heat oven to 300 degrees. Peel potato. Using a mandoline, slice potato lengthwise into 24 1/16-inch thick slices, stacking them to prevent from drying out.
2. Line 2 baking sheets with parchment paper; rub each with canola oil. Arrange potato slices on baking sheets, spacing them apart and turn them in the oil to coat. Lightly sprinkle with salt and bake, rotating sheets and flipping potato slices every 5 minutes, until crisp and browned, 40 to 50 minutes. Some will brown faster than others. Transfer potato crisps to a paper towel lined plate. Pat dry with a paper towel; set aside.
3. Cut salmon into ⅛-inch cubes. Transfer to a bowl and add Dijon mustard, cornichons, onions ,capers and olive oil, and season with salt and pepper to taste.
4. Fold in parsley and chives. Chill for 30 minutes. Serve tartare on potato crisps garnished with chopped chives.

Wild Mushroom Confit on Crostini with Brie and Truffle Oil

One baguette, thinly sliced and toasted in a 400 degree oven until golden brown
3 tablespoons olive oil
1 12-ounce package chopped crimini mushrooms
½ ounce dried porcini mushrooms, rehydrated in boiling water, (save water)
1 small shallot, minced
2 cloves garlic, minced
2 teaspoons chopped fresh sage
2 teaspoon chopped fresh parsley
Salt and freshly ground black pepper
Pinch of red pepper flakes
1 wedge Brie
Truffle oil for drizzling

Makes 10 Crostini

1. Place the chopped mushrooms in the food processor and pulse until coarsely ground. Rehydrate the porcinis until soft. Squeeze dry and chop.
2. Heat the olive oil in a skillet and add the shallots and garlic. Sauté until soft. Add the mushrooms and sauté until lightly browned. Add a little of the porcini liquid and the fresh herbs. Season with salt and pepper and red pepper flakes. Continue to cook until almost dry.
3. Place a thin slice of Brie on each crostini. Top with a tablespoon of the mushroom confit.
4. Preheat the oven to 375 degrees. Bake the crostini just until the cheese melts and is warm.
5. Remove and place on a serving tray. Drizzle with some of the truffle oil.

Goat Cheese Mousse with Cranberry Chutney

1 envelope unflavored gelatin
¾ cup plain Greek yogurt
½ cup quark (if not available, substitute 4 ounces ricotta cheese blended with 1 tablespoon sour cream)
2 ounces soft goat cheese
3 tablespoons fresh chives
Salt to taste
Freshly ground black pepper
¾ cup heavy cream
Sweet pepper or cranberry chutney
Crackers or toasted French baguette

Makes About 4 Cups

1. Sprinkle gelatin over ½ cup water in a small saucepan; let stand 1 minute. Cook 2 minutes over low heat, stirring until gelatin dissolves.
2. Whisk together gelatin mixture, yogurt, quark and goat cheese in a large bowl. Stir in the chives. Season with salt and pepper.
3. Beat cream in a separate chilled bowl until soft peaks form. Fold gently into cheese mixture. Cover and chill 3 hours. Serve with the chutney, crackers or toasted baguette.

Endive with Boursin Cheese & Honey-Glazed Pecans

¾ cup pecan halves
2 tablespoons honey
Boursin cheese
Endive

Makes 3 Dozen

1. Preheat the oven to 350 degrees. Line a baking sheet with parchment paper. In a small bowl, toss the pecans with the honey. Place them in a single layer on a baking sheet. Bake for 5 minutes; then stir and continue baking until shiny, about 4 minutes. Set aside to cool.
2. Using a pastry bag place some of the Boursin cheese in the large part of the endive leaf. Place one of the pecans on top of the cheese.
3. Serve on a large tray.

This easy hors d'oeuvre is great with champagne.

Green Tapenade

2 cloves garlic, coarsely chopped
⅔ cup slivered almonds, lightly toasted
3 tablespoons capers, drained
3 anchovy fillets, drained
2 cups pitted green olives, such as Picholine
⅓ cup brandy or Armagnac
½ cup olive oil
¼ cup slivered fresh basil
Freshly ground black pepper to taste

Makes 24

1. Place the garlic, almonds, capers, anchovies, olives and Armagnac in a food processor and process until the mixture is coarsely ground.
2. With the machine running, slowly pour the olive oil through the feed tube to bind the mixture into textured spread. Mix in the basil and season the tapenade with pepper.
3. Transfer the tapenade to a bowl, cover and place in the refrigerator for a few hours before serving. Serve tapenade at room temperature surrounded by toasted rounds of French bread.

Wild Mushroom Boxes

1. Preheat the oven to 375 degrees. Line a baking sheet with parchment paper.
2. On a lightly floured work surface, lay 1 sheet of puff pastry, brush with the beaten egg, and cut into nine 3 ⅓-inch squares. Place the squares of puff pastry on the baking sheet. Lightly perforate the second sheet of pastry with the tines of a fork and cut it into 9 squares also. Place each of these, perforated side up, on top of an egg-brushed square.
3. Using just the tip of a small sharp knife, outline a 2 ⅓-inch square cutout within the top square of pastry only, taking care not to cut all the way through. This will leave a ½ -inch frame in the perforated piece. Do not remove the square you outlined.
4. Bake until puffy and golden brown and the cut section is bursting out, for about 15-20 minutes. The pastry will resemble boxes. Remove from the oven, allow the pastry to cool on racks, and carefully remove the cutouts, or lids, with the tip of a sharp knife.
5. While the pastry is baking, heat the oil in a large skillet over high heat. When the oil is hot, add the mushrooms, salt and pepper, and sauté for about 5 minutes. Add the green onions, shallots and garlic and sauté for 1 minute. Stir in the beef glaze and simmer for 3 minutes. Fold in the butter and cook just until the butter is incorporated, for about 1 minute. Remove from the heat.
6. To serve, place a pastry box on each plate. Spoon some of the mushroom filling into each box, place 2 chives on top of each and replace the lids, letting the chives stick out.

2 10 inch-square sheets frozen puff pastry, thawed
1 large egg, lightly beaten
2 tablespoons olive oil
4 cups sliced assorted fresh wild mushrooms, such as shiitakes, chanterelles, morels, portabellas or porcini
1 ½ teaspoons salt
8 turns freshly ground black pepper
½ cup chopped green onions
1 tablespoon minced shallots
1 tablespoon minced garlic
1 ½ cups beef glaze (stock reduced until very thick)
2 teaspoons unsalted butter, at room temperature
8 whole fresh chives

Makes 9 Boxes

The mushroom boxes can be served for lunch with a salad or as a first course.

Grilled Shrimp Skewers with Red Curry Peanut Sauce

2 tablespoons vegetable oil
½ cup minced green onions
1 tablespoon minced peeled fresh ginger
2 garlic cloves, minced
2 tablespoons Thai red curry paste
¾ cup smooth peanut butter
1 cup canned unsweetened coconut milk
½ cup (or more) chicken broth
1 tablespoon sugar or honey
1 tablespoon soy sauce
½ teaspoon freshly ground black pepper
2 ½ tablespoons fresh lime juice
½ cup chopped fresh cilantro

1 ½ pounds large Tiger prawns
Skewers

Serves 8 - 10

1. Preheat the grill. Toss the prawns with some olive oil and thread 1 or 2 of the shrimp on the skewers and place on a very hot grill for about 1 ½ minutes on each side.
2. To make the sauce heat the oil in a saucepan over medium heat. Add the green onions, ginger and garlic; sauté for 2 minutes. Add curry paste; stir 1 minute. Whisk in peanut butter, then the coconut milk, broth, sugar, soy sauce and black pepper; bring to a boil. Reduce the heat to medium; simmer until reduced to 2 cups, whisking and adding more broth as needed, about 5 minutes. Remove from the heat and cool. Stir in the lime juice. Rewarm the sauce, thinning with broth.
3. Place the shrimp skewers on a large platter or remove the skewers and serve the shrimp with the sauce.

SPRING

Crab and Corn Beignets with Herbed Mayonnaise

1. Char the red pepper under the broiler, turning frequently, until blackened and blistered on all sides. Transfer the pepper to a zip-lock bag and cool for about 10 minutes. Discard the blackened skin, stem and seeds and cut the pepper into ¼-inch dice.

2. In a large bowl, whisk the flour with the cornmeal, baking powder, ¾ teaspoon of salt and ¼ teaspoon of pepper. Stir in the milk and egg. Fold in the crabmeat, corn kernels, scallion and diced red pepper. Let the batter rest for 10 minutes.

3. In the bowl of a mini prep, blend the mayonnaise with the basil, cilantro, lemon juice, tarragon, mustard and season with salt and pepper.

4. Preheat the oven to 300 degrees. Have ready a rack set over a baking sheet. In a large skillet, heat 1 ½ inches of oil to 350 degrees. Cook the beignets without crowding the pan; drop rounded teaspoons of the batter into the hot oil and fry until golden, about 1 minute per side. Drain on the rack and keep warm in the oven while you fry the rest. Repeat with the remaining batter, adjusting the heat if the beignets brown too quickly. Transfer the beignets to a platter and serve with the herbed mayonnaise.

1 small red bell pepper
½ cup all-purpose flour
2 tablespoons cornmeal
½ teaspoon baking powder
Salt and freshly ground pepper
⅓ cup milk
1 large egg, lightly beaten
½ pound crabmeat, picked over
½ cup fresh corn kernels
1 scallion, minced

HERBED MAYONNAISE
½ cup mayonnaise
1 tablespoon chopped basil
1 tablespoon chopped cilantro
1 tablespoon fresh lemon juice
½ teaspoon chopped tarragon
1 teaspoon Dijon mustard
Vegetable oil for frying

Makes 40 Beignets

1. Combine the sour cream and chives in small bowl. Cover and refrigerate.
2. Cut kernels from the ear of corn. Scrape remaining pulp from cob using the dull side of a knife blade. Discard cob. Set corn aside.
3. Lightly spoon flour into a dry measuring cup. Combine flour and cornmeal in a medium bowl; make a well in the center of mixture.
4. Combine milk and egg yolk in a small bowl; stir well with a whisk. Add milk mixture to flour mixture, and stir with a whisk just until moist. Stir in corn, salt and pepper.
5. Place the egg white in a bowl; beat with a mixer at high speed until foamy. Gently fold egg white into the corn mixture.
6. Heat a large nonstick skillet over medium heat. Coat pan with cooking spray. Spoon about 1 tablespoon batter per blini onto pan, spreading to about 2-inch diameter. Cook 2 minutes or until tops are covered with bubbles and edges begin to set. Carefully turn blinis over, cook for 1 minute longer.
7. Transfer blinis to a serving platter, and arrange in a single layer; keep warm. Repeat process with the remaining batter. Top each blini with 1 piece salmon and 1 teaspoon sour cream. Garnish with chopped chives.

½ cup sour cream
1 tablespoon minced fresh chives
1 ear corn
⅓ cup all purpose flour
2 tablespoons fine-ground yellow cornmeal
½ cup milk
1 large egg yolk
¼ teaspoon salt
¼ teaspoon black pepper
⅛ teaspoon cayenne
1 large egg white
Cooking spray
4 ounces smoked salmon, cut into 24 strips
Chopped fresh chives

Makes 24

Artichoke & Poblano Quesadillas

1 large clove garlic, peeled
2 (6-ounce) jars marinated artichoke hearts, drained
6 large basil leaves, cut into chiffonade
6 (8-inch) flour tortillas
2 cups grated pepper jack cheese
1 poblano chile, roasted, peeled and cut into thin strips

Serves 6

1. With a food processor running, add the garlic clove through
   the feed tube until it is finely chopped. Add the drained
   artichoke hearts and the basil; pulse until mixture is finely
   chopped.
2. Spread half of each tortilla with a few tablespoons of the
   artichoke mixture. Sprinkle about ⅓ cup of the grated
   cheese over the artichoke spread. Arrange a few strips of
   chile over the cheese. Fold tortillas in half and brush both
   sides with a little olive oil.
3. Heat a large non-stick skillet over medium high heat. Put
   2 to 3 quesadillas into the skillet and cook until one side is
   lightly browned, about 2 minutes. Turn each quesadilla over
   and cook until golden, another 2 to 3 minutes. Remove
   from the skillet and cut into 4 to 6 wedges. Repeat with
   remaining quesadillas.

Grilled Smoked Salmon Pizza

1 pound prepared pizza dough, at room temperature
All-purpose flour
Olive oil
1 ½ cups mascarpone cheese, stirred until smooth
¾ pound thinly sliced smoked salmon
3 tablespoons capers, drained
¼ cup fresh chives
Lemon wedges

Serves 8

1. Cut the dough into 2 pieces, and dust lightly with flour. Roll out one piece on a well-floured surface, forming a circle about 6 to 7 inches in diameter. Leave the dough a little thicker around the edges to form a rim. Place on a piece of lightly oiled parchment paper. Repeat with second round of dough.
2. Brush one side of each dough round with olive oil, and place, oil sides down, on the grill. Grill for about 3 minutes or until bottom sides are browned and crisp. Lightly brush tops of dough with oil, and turn. Cook for about 3 more minutes. Remove to a cookie sheet or a large flat serving platter.
3. Spread grilled dough pieces evenly with mascarpone cheese. Top with smoked salmon, and sprinkle with capers and fresh chives.
4. Serve pizzas with lemon wedges.

Fontina and Tomato Squares with Basil

1. In a food processor, blend together the butter, cream cheese, salt and thyme. Add the flour and process until the dough comes together. Pat the dough into a rectangle, wrap in wax paper and refrigerate for 30 minutes.
2. Preheat oven to 375 degrees. On a lightly floured work surface, roll out the dough ¼ inch thick. Cut into an 18 x 14 inch rectangle and carefully fit it into a 16 x 12 inch sheet pan, pressing the dough up the sides. Bake the pastry for 20 - 25 minutes, until golden brown and cooked through. Remove from the oven and let cool slightly. Leave the oven on.
3. Brush the mustard over the cooled pastry. Arrange the sliced tomatoes in a single layer on the pastry. Sprinkle with the grated Fontina and shredded basil and drizzle the olive oil over all. Season with coarse salt and pepper and bake for about 20 minutes, until the cheese is bubbling. Cut the pastry into 40 squares.
4. Serve at room temperature or warm.

PASTRY
2 sticks butter, at room temperature
8 ounces cream cheese,
at room temperature
1 teaspoon salt
1 teaspoon thyme
2 cups flour

TOPPING
3 tablespoons Dijon mustard
5 ripe medium tomatoes, thinly sliced
3 cups coarsely grated Italian Fontina cheese (6 ounces)
3 tablespoons finely shredded fresh basil leaves
2 tablespoons olive oil
Coarse (kosher) salt
Freshly ground pepper

Makes 40 hors d'oeuvres

1 pound lump crabmeat
1 red bell pepper, cored, seeded and minced
2 scallions, trimmed and minced
1 jalapeno pepper, cored, seeded and minced
Grated zest and juice of 1 lemon
¼ cup mayonnaise
2 cups fresh bread crumbs
2 large egg whites
½ teaspoon salt
½ teaspoon freshly ground black pepper
A pinch of cayenne pepper
6 basil leaves, cut into thin strips
¼ cup melted butter
½ cup Cajun Aioli
1 lemon, cut into wedges
Butter lettuce, leaves separated

CAJUN AIOLI

1 red bell pepper, roasted, peeled, cored and seeded
1 jalapeno pepper, roasted, peeled, cored and seeded
5 roasted garlic cloves
1 large egg
Juice of 1 lemon
½ teaspoon sea salt
¼ teaspoon freshly ground black pepper
¼ teaspoon cayenne pepper
¾ cup canola oil

Serves 6

Crab Cakes with Cajun Aioli in Lettuce Cup

1. Preheat the oven to 400 degrees.
2. Place the crabmeat in a bowl. Add the bell pepper, scallions, jalapeno pepper, lemon zest and juice, mayonnaise, 1 ½ cups bread crumbs, egg whites, salt, black pepper, cayenne pepper and basil and stir gently to mix.
3. Place the remaining bread crumbs on a plate. Scoop the crabmeat with an ice cream scoop and pat it out to form a cake about 2 inches around and 1 ½ inches thick. Roll the cake in the bread crumbs to coat lightly on both sides and shake gently to remove any excess crumbs. Place the crab cakes on a parchment lined tray and repeat with the remaining crabmeat mixture to form additional cakes.
4. Drizzle the melted butter over the crab cakes. Place in the preheated oven for about 20 minutes until golden brown. Serve placed inside a lettuce cup with the Cajun Aioli and lemon wedges.

CAJUN AIOLI

1. Place the bell pepper, jalapeno pepper, garlic, egg , lemon juice, salt, pepper and cayenne in the bowl of a food processor. Pulse to mix. With the motor of the food processor running, add the oil through the feed tube in a very thin, slow stream until it forms an emulsion. Add the remaining oil until all is incorporated.
2. Use the Aioli immediately or refrigerate in an airtight container for up to 4 days.

Spicy Cajun Shrimp Pâté

⅓ cup mayonnaise
1 3-ounce package cream cheese, cut into cubes
3 tablespoons chopped shallots
¾ pound cooked shrimp, well drained
1 tablespoon horseradish, grated
1 teaspoon Dijon mustard
1 teaspoon fresh dill
½ teaspoon sugar
½ teaspoon salt
1 tablespoon lemon juice
¼ teaspoon Tabasco
¼ teaspoon cayenne pepper

Makes 2 Cups

1. In a food processor, combine mayonnaise and cream cheese. Add remaining ingredients and mix until blended.
2. Shape into a ball. Refrigerate several hours or overnight for flavors to blend.
3. May be refrigerated up to 2 days. Do not freeze.
4. Serve pâté with crackers or bread rounds.

Grilled Eggplant and Tomato Sandwiches

3 large Japanese eggplants, each cut lengthwise into thirds
⅓ cup olive oil
2 large garlic cloves, minced
¼ cup chopped fresh basil plus
8 fresh basil leaves
24 4½-inch thick diagonal slices country-style bread
1 large tomato, cut into ¼ inch thick slices
4 slices Fontina cheese

Makes 24

1. Prepare barbecue. (medium high heat)
2. Sprinkle eggplant slices generously with salt. Let stand 5 minutes. Pat dry.
3. Combine oil, garlic and chopped basil in small bowl. Season with salt and pepper. Brush eggplant slices, bread and tomato slices with garlic oil.
4. Grill eggplant until very tender and slightly charred, turning frequently, about 7 minutes per side. Arrange bread and tomatoes on barbecue during last 3 minutes of eggplant-grilling time and cook until bread is golden and tomatoes begin to soften, about 1 minute per side.
5. Top each bread slice on grill with eggplant, cheese, tomato slices and whole basil leaves, dividing evenly. Season with salt and pepper. Cover grill until cheese just melts, about 1 minute. Transfer sandwiches to plates. Garnish with basil sprigs and serve.

Hot-Glazed Scallops

12 sea scallops, cut in half horizontally
Scallion greens, julienned and placed in ice water for 10 minutes, for garnish

MAYONNAISE
1 egg yolk
2 teaspoons Dijon mustard
¼ teaspoon cayenne pepper
Juice of one lemon
Salt and pepper
1 cup olive oil

Serves 6

1. Place 2 sliced scallops on scallop shells that have been sprayed with vegetable spray.
2. To make the mayonnaise, put all of the ingredients except the olive oil in a blender or the bowl of a food processor. Blend and then slowly add olive oil a drop at a time.
3. Spoon heaping tablespoons of the mayonnaise on each scallop shell.
4. Bake at 400 degrees for 12 to 14 minutes.
5. Garnish with scallion greens and serve.

If making your own mayonnaise will keep you from making this hors d'oeuvre, try this:
1 cup mayonnaise
2 teaspoons mustard
¼ teaspoon cayenne pepper
Juice of one lemon
Salt and pepper
Mix together until smooth.
Really good on any fish!

1. Bring the butter, water and salt to a boil in a small heavy saucepan. Add the flour and stir until the mixture forms into a ball and pulls away from the sides of the pan. Transfer to a bowl and cool slightly. Add the egg and cayenne pepper, then fold in the mashed potatoes. Add the crab until completely mixed together. Put the panko in the bowl of a food processor and grind until very fine.
2. Form the crab mixture into a log and roll in the panko breadcrumbs. Cut into 1 ½ inch pieces.
3. Heat the canola oil until very hot, and cook the tater tots for about 3 minutes until golden brown. Drain on paper towels and serve with chipotle mayonnaise.

CHIPOTLE MAYONNAISE

Mix all of the ingredients together in the bowl of a mini prep until smooth. Taste for seasoning.

2 tablespoons unsalted butter, cut into pieces
¼ cup water
Pinch of salt
¼ cup all-purpose flour
1 egg
1 cup mashed potatoes
¼ teaspoon cayenne pepper
½ pound lump crabmeat
Salt and freshly ground pepper

Panko bread crumbs
Canola Oil

CHIPOTLE MAYONNAISE
1 cup mayonnaise
1 chipotle chile
1 clove garlic, grated
Juice of 1 lime

Makes 16

Fried Ravioli Bites with Spicy Marinara

1 package four cheese ravioli, prepared according to package directions
2 large eggs, beaten
1 cup Italian dry bread crumbs
1-2 cup freshly grated Parmesan cheese
Canola oil
1 32-ounce can Toscana Sauce, seasoned with oregano and red pepper flakes.

Makes 30 Ravioli Bites

1. Prepare the ravioli according to package directions. Mix the bread crumbs and Parmesan cheese together.
2. Dip prepared ravioli into beaten eggs, coating both sides, then into bread crumbs, coating both sides. Place on prepared baking sheet.
3. Heat the sauce.
4. Heat the oil until 375 degrees. Fry the ravioli until crispy on both sides. Serve with the marinara sauce.

Toscana sauce is a prepared marinara. Any that you like is great, just add red pepper flakes and oregano.

Grilled Sea Scallop Nachos with Avocado Puree and Jalapeno Pesto

1. Heat the grill to high. Brush the scallops on both sides with the oil and season with salt and pepper.
2. Grill for about 3 to 4 minutes per side.
3. Spread about one tablespoon of the avocado puree over each chip. Top the puree with a scallop and top each scallop with a dollop of the pesto. Garnish with cilantro leaves.

AVOCADO PUREE
Combine all of the ingredients in a food processor and process until combined, but a little chunky. Puree until smooth.

JALAPENO PESTO
Combine cilantro, jalapeno, garlic, pine nuts, salt and pepper in a food processor and process until coarsely chopped. With the motor running, slowly add the oil and process until emulsified. Scrape into a bowl.

Grilled shrimp also very good.

20 large sea scallops
Olive Oil
Salt and pepper
Corn tortilla chips
Cilantro leaves

AVOCADO PUREE
1 ripe avocado, peeled and chopped
2 tablespoons chopped red onion
2 limes, juiced
2 tablespoons olive oil
¼ cup chopped fresh cilantro leaves
Salt and pepper to taste

JALAPENO PESTO
1 ½ cups cilantro leaves
4 jalapenos, grilled and chopped
1 clove garlic, chopped
2 tablespoons pine nuts
Salt and pepper
½ cup olive oil

Makes 20 Nachos

Spicy Sweet Potato Fries with
Smoked Chile-Buttermilk Sauce and Blue Cheese

1 package frozen sweet potato French fries, cooked
according to package instructions
Ancho chile powder for sprinkling

SMOKED CHILE-BUTTERMILK SAUCE WITH BLUE
CHEESE
¼ cup sour cream
1 cup buttermilk
2 cloves garlic, grated
2 tablespoons finely chopped red onion
1 tablespoon lime juice
2 teaspoons chipotle puree
½ cup crumbled blue cheese
Salt and pepper to taste

Serves 10

1. To make the sauce combine all of the ingredients in a small
   bowl. Refrigerate at least 30 minutes before serving.
2. Take the sweet potato fries out of the oven and place them in
   parchment paper cones. Sprinkle with ancho chile powder.
3. Serve with the smoked Chile-buttermilk sauce.

Perfect (Spicy) Bloody Mary with Celery Spears

1 ½ cups tomato juice
4 ounces vodka
Juice of 1 lemon
2 tablespoons prepared horseradish, drained
2 to 4 dashes hot sauce
2 dashes Worcestershire sauce
¼ teaspoon celery salt
¼ teaspoon freshly ground black pepper
Ice cubes
Celery spears and jalapeño chiles for garnish

Serves 2

1. Whisk together the tomato juice, vodka, lemon juice, horse-radish, hot sauce, Worcestershire, celery salt, and pepper in a small pitcher, and refrigerate until cold, at least 30 minutes.
2. Pour the mixture into 2 large glasses filled with ice and garnish each with a celery spear and a jalapeño.

Smoked Salmon, Wasabi and Pickled Ginger Tartines

½ seedless cucumber
1 tablespoon wasabi paste (from a tube)
4 ounces cream cheese, softened
1 baguette, quartered crosswise, then each quarter halved
horizontally and lightly toasted
½ pound thinly sliced smoked salmon
¼ cup bottled pickled ginger, drained
Lemon wedges

Serves 8

1. Cut cucumber into thin rounds using a slicer. Stir together
   wasabi and cream cheese. Spread mixture on baguette, and then
   make open-face sandwiches with cucumber, salmon and ginger.
2. Garnish with lemon wedges and micro greens.

Lobster Corn Dogs with Tarragon-Mustard Sauce

TARRAGON-MUSTARD SAUCE

1 cup mayonnaise

¼ cup Dijon mustard

2 tablespoons chopped fresh chives

2 teaspoons dry mustard

2 dashes of Worcestershire sauce

2 dashes of hot pepper sauce

salt and pepper to taste

CORN DOGS

8 ounces uncooked medium shrimp, peeled, deveined

½ teaspoon salt

1 large egg

2 tablespoons heavy cream

1 teaspoon Worcestershire sauce

¾ teaspoon Cajun seasoning

½ teaspoon Crystal hot sauce

1 pound cooked lobster meat, cut into ¼-inch cubes (about 4 cups)

1 ear of corn, kernels removed

½ cup thinly sliced green onions

12 corn dog sticks

BATTER

1 cup all-purpose flour

¼ cup cornmeal

1 teaspoon salt

¼ teaspoon smoked paprika

1 cup lager beer

Peanut oil for frying

Makes 12

Indulgent to be sure, but a very delicious re-make on the corn dog.

1. Whisk all of the ingredients for the sauce in a medium bowl to blend. Season to taste with salt and pepper.
2. Using on/off turns, blend the shrimp and salt in a food processor until coarsely chopped. Add the egg, cream, Worcestershire sauce, Cajun seasoning and hot pepper sauce. Process until smooth. Mix the lobster, corn and green onions in a large bowl. Add shrimp puree; fold in until blended.
3. Divide mixture into 12 equal portions (about $^1/_3$ cup). Using moistened hands, form each into 3 x 1 ½ -inch log and place on a baking sheet. Insert the corn dog stick into 1 end of each log, pushing through almost to other end. Cover and chill at least 4 hours and up to 6 hours.
4. Whisk first 4 ingredients for the batter in a medium bowl. Whisk in the beer.
5. Add enough oil to a heavy large saucepan to reach a depth of 3 inches. Heat the oil to 350 degrees. Dip 1 corn dog into the batter; turn to coat corn dog plus ½ inch of stick. Let float in hot oil. Repeat with 3 more corn dogs. Fry until golden brown and crisp, and centers are cooked through, occasionally grasping sticks with tongs to turn carefully, 4 to 5 minutes. Transfer to paper towels to drain. Repeat in 2 more batches with remaining corn dogs and batter. Serve with the sauce.

Feta with Piquillo Pepper & Chive Oil

1. Combine the roasted peppers with 1 tablespoon oil and season with salt and pepper to taste; cover and let marinate for 30 minutes at room temperature.
2. Toss pita wedges with 2 tablespoons oil in a bowl; season with salt and pepper. Spread pita wedges out in a single layer on a baking sheet and bake until just golden and crisp, 7-8 minutes. Keep warm.
3. Place the olive oil and chives in a blender and blend until smooth. Strain and reserve.
4. Arrange feta cubes on a tray. Top with red peppers, micro greens and gently press a pita chip or tortilla chip into the cheese. Drizzle a little of the chive oil around the cheese.

1 Piquillo pepper, cut into small dice
3 tablespoons olive oil divided
¼ cup chopped chives
3-4 pieces of pita bread, cut into wedges, or tortilla chips
Salt and freshly ground black pepper
6 1½-inch cubes feta
2 tablespoons micro greens

Serves 6

Piquillo peppers are readily available and are very sweet. They pair well with the feta cheese and red pepper flakes.

Crab Rangoon

1. In a small skillet, cook the onions, garlic and ginger until soft. Remove from the heat.
2. In a bowl, combine the cooked onion mixture, cream cheese, goat cheese, soy sauce, hot sauce, green onions and cilantro and blend together. Add the Monterey Jack and mix well. Fold in the crabmeat. Adjust the seasoning to taste.
3. Working 1 at a time, place the wonton wrappers on a work surface. Spoon about ¼ cup of the mixture into the center of the wrapper and wet the edges. Fold over the sides to form a triangle and press to seal the edges. Set on a baking sheet and cover with a lightly damp cloth to prevent from drying out while assembling the remaining ingredients.
4. Heat a large sauté pan over medium-high heat. When the pan is hot, add the oil and swirl to coat the pan. Add the crab rangoons and brown on both sides, about 2 minutes per side. Once the rangoons are well browned, add a little water and cover. Cook an additional 2 minutes.
5. Arrange on a plate and sprinkle with the Creole seasoning.

¼ cup minced onions
1 tablespoon minced garlic
1 tablespoon minced ginger
8 ounces cream cheese, softened
4 ounces goat cheese, softened
2 teaspoons soy sauce
½ teaspoon Crystal hot sauce
¼ cup chopped green onions
1 tablespoon fresh cilantro leaves
2 ounces Monterey Jack cheese, grated
1 pound lump crabmeat
1 package wonton wrappers
Water
Vegetable oil
Creole seasoning for garnish

Makes 2 Dozen

Serve with a store-bought garlic-chile sauce.

Rosemary Cheese Crackers

2 cups grated sharp Cheddar Cheese
1 stick unsalted butter, room temperature
1 ½ cups all-purpose flour
2 teaspoons fresh rosemary
1 teaspoon salt
1 teaspoon crushed red pepper flakes
¼ teaspoon ground cayenne pepper

Makes About 2 ½ Dozen 2-Inch Crackers

1. Cream the cheese and butter together in the bowl of a food processor until smooth and well combined. Add the flour, rosemary, salt, red pepper flakes and cayenne. Pulse until the mixture forms into a ball.
2. Turn the dough onto a piece of parchment paper. Roll into a log. Wrap the dough in the paper and refrigerate for several hours or overnight.
3. Preheat the oven to 375 degrees.
4. Remove the dough from the refrigerator. Cut the log into ¼-inch thick slices and arrange them on a baking sheet. Using a fork, prick the center of each cracker several times and sprinkle with salt. Bake for 12 to 15 minutes, until golden brown around the edges.
5. Remove from the oven and allow to cool before serving.

6 long, fairly thick asparagus spears, stems peeled
Freshly ground pepper
9 thin slices of lean prosciutto (2-3 ounces)
6 sheets of phyllo dough
3 tablespoons unsalted butter, melted
½ cup freshly grated Parmesan
Ground nutmeg

Makes 6 Crispy Rolls

1. In a saucepan of boiling water, blanch the asparagus until crisp-tender, about 2 minutes. Refresh under cold water and pat very dry with paper towels.
2. Season the asparagus spears with pepper. Roll them in the prosciutto; you will need about 1 ½ slices to cover each spear.
3. Lay 1 sheet of the phyllo on a work surface with the short end directly in front of you. Brush it with butter and sprinkle with 1 tablespoon of the Parmesan cheese and a pinch of nutmeg. Set a wrapped asparagus on the short end of the phyllo and roll it up snugly. Brush the roll with butter, dust it lightly with more Parmesan and set it on a baking sheet. Repeat with the remaining ingredients, arranging the rolls at least 2 inches apart on the sheet.
4. Preheat the oven to 400 degrees. Bake the rolls on the top shelf of the oven for 10 to 12 minutes, or until golden brown and crisp. Let the rolls cool slightly before serving. Serve on a bed of grated Parmesan.

AIOLI A strong flavored garlic mayonnaise from the Provence region of Southern France. It is a popular accompaniment for fish, meats and vegetables.

ANCHO CHILE This broad dried chile is 3 to 4 inches long and a deep reddish brown. It ranges in flavor from mild to pungent. This rich, slightly fruit-flavored ancho is the sweetest of the dried chiles. In its fresh green state, the ancho is called a poblano chile.

BEIGNETS The name comes from the French word for "fritter".

BOCCONCINI A small nugget of fresh mozzarella. It is Italian for "mouthful".

CHIPOTLE This hot chile is a dried, smoked Jalapeno. It has a wrinkled, dark brown skin and a smoky, sweet, almost chocolaty flavor. Chipotles can be found dried, pickled and canned in adobo sauce.

GAZPACHO A refreshingly cold, summertime soup from the Andalusia region in southern Spain. This uncooked soup is usually made from a pureed mixture of fresh tomatoes, sweet bell peppers, onions, celery, cucumber, garlic, olive oil, vinegar and lemon juice.

GELATIN An odorless, tasteless and colorless thickening agent, which when dissolved in hot water and then cooled, forms a jelly.

HAVARTI The flavor of young Havarti cheese is mild yet tangy. As it ages the flavor intensifies and sharpens.

MANCHEGO Spain's most famous cheese, Manchego is a rich, golden, semi firm cheese. It has a full, mellow flavor.

OUZO From Greece, this clear, sweet anise-flavored liqueur is usually served as an aperitif. It's generally mixed with water which turns it whitish and opaque.

PESTO Italian for "pounded", pesto is an uncooked sauce made with fresh basil, garlic, pine nuts, Parmesan cheese and olive oil.

POBLANO A dark green chile with a rich flavor that varies from mild to snappy.

REMOULADE This classic French sauce is made by combining mayonnaise with mustard, capers, chopped gherkins, herbs and anchovies. It is served chilled as an accompaniment to cold meat, fish and shellfish.

TAHINI Used in Middle Eastern cooking, tahini is a thick paste made of ground sesame seed. It is used to flavor hummus.

TOMATILLO This fruit, also called a Mexican green tomato belongs to the same family. The papery husk is a clue to the fact that the tomatillo is also related to the Cape gooseberry.

WASABI Japanese version of horseradish that comes from the root of an Asian plant. Used to make a green-colored condiment that has a sharp, pungent, fiery flavor. It is available in both a paste and powder.

Index